P9-DNI-389

INVINCIBLE
IRON MAN
IRONHEART

w Iron Man?. (Sub
24,203,800 views
cribe
334,776 12,6
654 22722 4075
NEW YORK'S FINEST NEWSPAPER
IRONHEART?
Sed varius tincidunt sem, ut consequat diam dictum a. Vestibulum pulvinar arcu a dolor vestibulum sodales. Suspendisse imperdiet luctus est, sed luctus arcu posuere vitae. Praesent elementum eleifend tincidunt. Nunc quis elit id neque pretium congue. Praesent magna lacus, egestas non porttitor vitae, venenatis nec purus. Aenean tristique, sem at tincidunt tempor, ante nisl rhoncus arcu, nec interdum nunc tellus ac est. Aenean felis dui, molestie non dictum et, mollis non leo. Donec quam orci, auctor eu accumsan non, pulvinar egestas lorem. Nulla congue tincidunt nibh vel pulvinar. Vestibulum dignissim nibh sit amet libero sollicitudin placerat. Maecenas facilisis erat non turpis lobortis porta orci suscipit.
IRONHEART TAKES DOWN MYSTERY ASSAILANT

INVINCIBLE IRON MAN IRONHEART

CHOICES

BRIAN MICHAEL BENDIS
WRITER

STEFANO CASELLI WITH
KATE NIEMCZYK (#11), **TAKI SOMA** (#11) & **KIICHI MIZUSHIMA** (#11)
ARTISTS

MARTE GRACIA WITH **ISRAEL SILVA** (#9-10),
COLOR ARTISTS

VC's CLAYTON COWLES
LETTERER

STEFANO CASELLI &
MARTE GRACIA (#6-8, #10),
DANIEL ACUÑA (#9) AND
JESÚS SAIZ (#11)
COVER ART

ALANNA SMITH
ASSISTANT EDITOR

TOM BREVOORT
EDITOR

IRON MAN CREATED BY
STAN LEE, LARRY LIEBER,
DON HECK & JACK KIRBY

COLLECTION EDITOR: **JENNIFER GRÜNWALD**
ASSISTANT EDITOR: **CAITLIN O'CONNELL**
ASSOCIATE MANAGING EDITOR: **KATERI WOODY**
EDITOR, SPECIAL PROJECTS: **MARK D. BEAZLEY**
VP PRODUCTION & SPECIAL PROJECTS: **JEFF YOUNGQUIST**
SVP PRINT, SALES & MARKETING: **DAVID GABRIEL**
BOOK DESIGNER: **ADAM DEL RE**

EDITOR IN CHIEF: **AXEL ALONSO**
CHIEF CREATIVE OFFICER: **JOE QUESADA**
PRESIDENT: **DAN BUCKLEY**
EXECUTIVE PRODUCER: **ALAN FINE**

INVINCIBLE IRON MAN: IRONHEART VOL. 2 — CHOICES. Contains material originally published in magazine form as INVINCIBLE IRON MAN #6-11. First printing 2017. ISBN# 978-1-302-90673-3. Published by MARVEL WORLDWIDE, INC., a subsidiary of MARVEL ENTERTAINMENT, LLC. OFFICE OF PUBLICATION: 135 West 50th Street, New York, NY 10020. DAN BUCKLEY, President, Marvel Entertainment; JOE QUESADA, Chief Creative Officer; TOM BREVOORT, SVP of Publishing; DAVID BOGART, SVP of Business Affairs & Operations, Publishing & Partnership; C.B. CEBULSKI, VP of Brand Management & Development, Asia; DAVID GABRIEL, SVP of Sales & Marketing, Publishing; JEFF YOUNGQUIST, VP of Production & Special Projects; DAN CARR, Executive Director of Publishing Technology; ALEX MORALES, Director of Publishing Operations; SUSAN CRESPI, Production Manager; STAN LEE, Chairman Emeritus. For information regarding advertising in Marvel Comics or on Marvel.com, please contact Vit DeBellis, Integrated Sales Manager, at vdebellis@marvel.com. For Marvel subscription inquiries, please call 888-511-5480. **Manufactured between 10/27/2017 and 11/28/2017 by LSC COMMUNICATIONS INC., KENDALLVILLE, IN, USA.**

10 9 8 7 6 5 4 3 2 1

6

OKAY, IT'S OFFICIAL-- I, RIRI WILLIAMS, AM OFFICIALLY, BY ANYONE'S DEFINITION, A SUPER HERO.
IRONHEART.
NO, NOT IRON WOMAN. NO, NOT IRON MAIDEN, WHICH IS A REFERENCE I HAD TO LOOK UP...
NOT WHAT AN IRON MAIDEN **IS**, BUT WHAT THE **BAND** IRON MAIDEN WAS.
IRONHEART.
I'M BEING TRAINED AND ASSISTED BY TONY STARK'S ARTIFICIAL INTELLIGENCE, AND I JUST HAD A LEGITIMATE SUPER HERO TEAM-UP WITH NONE OTHER THAN PEPPER POTTS.
YEAH, YOU HEARD ME... **RESCUE.**
AND I DIDN'T COMPLETELY EMBARRASS MYSELF.
THEN I GOT AN EMAIL THIS MORNING, TELLING ME THAT I SHOULD FLY TO TONY STARK'S INDUSTRIAL COMPLEX IN DOVER, NEW JERSEY, BECAUSE TONY STARK'S MOTHER WANTS TO HAVE WORDS WITH ME.
SO, HOW'S YOUR WEEK BEEN?

TOLDJA.
I BELIEVED YOU, MISS POTTS.
RIRI, THE REASON WE WANTED TO TALK TO YOU IS--
THE MARK 7!
WOW.
THE SILVER CENTURION ARMOR!
ARE YOU KIDDING ME?
IS SHE RIGHT?
I'M GOING TO ASSUME SO.
TONY CALLED HIMSELF THE SILVER CENTURION AT ONE POINT?
THAT IS SO MUCH WORSE THAN IRON MAN.
I GET IT. I WAS ONCE IN STELLA MCCARTNEY'S PERSONAL WARDROBE. IT WAS INTENSE.
RIGINALLY, THIS ARMOR SYSTEM WAS A PRESENT FOR JAMES RHODES.
ORIGINALLY.
BUT HE ENDED UP KEEPING IT SO E COULD USE IT GAINST OBADIAH STANE.
THAT ARMOR THERE KICKED THE IRON MONGER'S ASS!
THIS-- THIS IS RESPECT.
AND, OH, AND THAT'S THE MARK 9. AND IT'S RIGHT HERE. IT'S JUST SITTING HERE. LIKE, NO BIG DEAL!
ONLY THE MOST SOPHISTICATED ADVANCEMENTS IN PERSONALIZED ARMORED--
HEY, KID! WOULD YOU LIKE TO KNOW WHY WE INVITED YOU OVER?

TO MAKE ME FEEL LIKE CRAP ABOUT MY ARMOR DESIGN CHOICES?
NO.
YOU KNOW MISS MARY JANE WATSON?
YES. THAT IS WHO YOU ARE. HEY.
AND YOU KNOW FRIDAY...
I WORSHIP FRIDAY!
YOU ARE THE WHOLE THING, LADY.
YOUR CODING... MAN.
WHAT I'VE SEEN OF IT.
YOUR CODING IS--IS GORGEOUS!
I DON'T KNOW ABOUT THE REST OF YOU, BUT I LIKE HER BETTER THAN TONY.
HEY!
ABOUT WHAT HAPPENED WITH YOU AND PEPPER...
ACTUALLY, WHAT HAPPENED AFTER IS REALLY--
YEAH, ALL THAT. AFTER ALL THAT WITH THE FIGHT, THE NINJAS...IT ALL CAME OUT OF NOWHERE!

KID.
E REAL TONY.
NOT YOU, THE WEIRD CODED 'RSION HE LEFT LYING AROUND TO HAUNT US.
AM I NOT REAL? WHAT IS REAL?
E BUTTHOLE. ONE WITH THE 'THOLE IS THE REAL ONE.
FAIR ENOUGH.
AND YOU KNOW PEPPER?
SURE!
ME AND PEPPER POTTS! TOTALLY!
IT'S, LIKE, NO BIG DEAL THAT THE MAGICAL FAIRY TALE I INVENTED IN MY HEAD IS ACTUALLY PLAYING OUT RIGHT NOW IN FRONT OF ME.
VELL, YOU HAD) EXPECT SOME ATTENTION.
NO! I MEAN, SURE.
BUT IT'S NOT WHY I WANT TO DO THIS.
AND IT JUST--IT ALL--RIGHT OUT OF NOWHERE!
THAT'S WHERE IT COMES FROM.
ONE MOMENT YOU'RE DOING THIS THING YOU LOVE OUT OF PURE LOVE, AND THEN SUDDENLY...

New Iron Man?!
24,203,800 views
Subscribe
334,776
Tim Broveert
Fell in love! # cool
654
22722
4075
"YEAH, EXACTLY... SUDDENLY!"
FOX NEWS
"ONE MINUTE I'M TRAINING, AND THE NEXT MINUTE I AM STUPID FAMOUS.
BUG
NEW YORK'S FINEST NEWSPAPER
IRONHEART?
Sed varius tincidunt sem, ut consequat diam dictum a. Vestibulum pulvinar arcu a dolor vestibulum sodales. Suspendisse imperdiet luctus est, sed luctus arcu posuere vitae. Praesent elementum eleifend tincidunt. Nunc quis elit id neque pretium congue. Praesent magna lacus, egestas non porttitor vitae, venenatis nec purus. Aenean tristique, sem at tincidunt tempor, ante nisl rhoncus arcu, nec interdum nunc tellus ac est. Aenean felis dui, molestie non dictum et, mollis non leo. Donec quam orci, auctor eu accumsan non, pulvinar egestas lorem. Nulla congue tincidunt nibh vel pulvinar. Vestibulum dignissim nibh sit amet libero sollicitudin placerat. Maecenas facilisis erat non turpis lobortis
porta orci suscipit.
"THERE ARE SO MANY WEIRD RUMORS ABOUT ME.
"PEOPLE THINK I MIGHT *BE* TONY STARK.
"OR THAT HE CREATED ME TO COVER THE MESS OF THE SUPER HERO CIVIL WAR.
IRONHEART TAKES DOWN MYSTERY ASSAILANT

Exclusive
"THIS ONE GUY WITH GREEN HAIR WAS ON THE NEWS TALKING ABOUT ME LIKE WE WERE BEST FRIENDS, AND I'VE NEVER MET THE GUY.
"IT WAS FASCINATING.
Doc Samson
Super hero psychiatrist
LATE@NIGHT
"I HAVEN'T DONE ANY PRESS.
"I THOUGHT ABOUT IT, BUT I--I DON'T THINK I WANT TO.
"BECAUSE--THIS IS WEIRD TO SAY OUT LOUD, BUT-- IT DOESN'T SEEM REAL.
CHICAGO NEWS
"LIKE, AT ALL."

GOOD.
BECAUSE IT'S *NOT.*
RIGHT. THAT MAKES SENSE, THEN...
WELL, AFTER TALKING IT OVER WITH PEPPER AND THE GANG HERE...
WE WANTED TO TALK TO YOU ABOUT THIS LABORATORY.
WHAT ABOUT IT?
WOULD YOU FEEL MORE COMFORTABLE USING *THIS* LABORATORY AS YOUR BASE OF OPERATIONS?
THIS ONE?
THE ONE WE'RE STANDING IN?
YES.

THIS-- HIS IS LIKE-- THIS IS--
THIS S HOLY PACE!
I CAN SEE HOW YOU SEE IT THAT WAY...
...BUT, WHAT I'M THINKING IS, WITHOUT AN IRON MAN, THE WORLD IS NOT GOING TO BE AS SAFE AS IT COULD BE, RIGHT?
AND WE HAVE ALL THIS STUFF LYING AROUND...
...AND THEN WE HAVE YOU.
BUT PEPPER POTTS IS RESCUE.
I'M ALREADY BUSY WITH A HANDFUL OF VERY LARGE PROJECTS THAT I HAVE DEDICATED YEARS OF MY LIFE TO.
I HAVE MADE PROMISES AND COMMITMENTS THAT COULD REALLY HELP US ALL IN THE NOT-SO-NEAR FUTURE.
I NEVER BACK DOWN FROM THE ARMOR WHEN I HAVE TO, BUT I DON'T NEED TO DO ALL THAT.
NOT LIKE YOU.

DO I JUST--?
YES, YES...
...YOU ARE EXPECTED.

LATVERIA.

LATVERIA, SIR?
LATVERIA.
HOME OF DOCTOR DOOM.

I'M NOT SURE WHAT YOU'RE ASKING OF ME, SIR.
GET IT FOR US, WILL YOU?
GET WHAT?
LATVERIA.
THE WHOLE--I'M SORRY, THE WHOLE COUNTRY?
FIND OUT WHO OWNS IT AND FIND OUT WHAT IT WILL TAKE.
MAYBE YOU'RE NOT HEARING ME, MR. LUCKY.
BUT WHO OWNS THE--
THE PLACE IS IN TOTAL DISARRAY!
I'M SAYING, YOU GO IN THERE, TURN ON THE LIGHTS, OPEN THE SCHOOLS AND FEED THESE PEOPLE, AND THEY'LL GIVE IT TO YOU.
OH.
THAT IS AN ANGLE TO CONSIDER.
WHY?
WHY LATVERIA?
IT HAS A SPECIAL PLACE IN OUR HEARTS.

CHICAGO.

YOU HAVE TO **THINK** ABOUT IT?

I **STILL** HAVE TO THINK ABOUT IT.

THEY WERE **OFFERING YOU** THE KEYS TO THE KINGDOM!

AND I'M **GOING** TO THINK ABOUT IT.

YOU THINK YOU DON'T DESERVE IT.

DON'T PSYCHOANALYZE ME!

I HATE WHEN **REAL** PEOPLE TRY TO DO THAT TO ME...

WHY HAVE YOU SEEN THE HULK NAKED?
SOMETIMES THE PURPLE PANTS STRETCH WITH HIM AND, YOU KNOW, SOMETIMES THEY DON'T.

CAN WE PLAY "THE QUIET GAME" NOW?
THERE'S SOMEONE FROM M.I.T. TALKING TO YOUR MOTHER IN THE DRIVEWAY.

UH-OH.
THEY KNOW YOU AR IRONHEART.

AGH!
BECAUSE I USED MATERIAL FROM THE SCHOOL TO BUILD MY PROTOTYPE.
MAYBE SEND AN EDIBLE BOUQUET.
I MEANT TO WRITE THEM AN APOLOGY EMAIL!

WHAT DO YOU THINK THEY WANT?
TO DECLARE PROPRIETARY OWNERSHIP OF THE ARMOR COPYRIGHT...?

OH, HELL NO!
YOU BUILT IT ON SCHOOL PROPERTY WITH SCHOOL MATERIAL.
THAT'S--
A GOOD AND ARGUABLE POINT--
NOT--
--IN COURT.
HOW MUCH ARE EDIBLE BOUQUETS?

RIRI.

HI.
RIRI.
MY NAME IS DANA RICHARDSON.

JUST SO WE CAN CLEAR THE AIR: NO ONE IS ANGRY, NOBODY IS SUING ANYONE.
WHAT WAS DONE WAS DONE, AND WHAT WAS, WAS.

THE INSTITUTE HAS ASKED ME TO COME HERE AND TALK TO YOU ABOUT COMING BACK TO SCHOOL.
AFTER REVIEWING YOUR ACADEMIC HISTORY, WE REALIZED THAT NOT ENOUGH ATTENTION WAS BEING PAID TO YOUR SPECIFIC NEEDS.

WE UNDERSTAND THAT YOU BUILT YOUR FIRST ARMOR OUT OF SCHOLASTIC BOREDOM.
WE'D LIKE YOU TO COME BACK WITH THE FULL RESOURCES OF OUR ROBOTICS LABORATORIES...

...AND WE WOULD LIKE YOU TO CONTINUE YOUR WORK ON CAMPUS.

I CAN OFFER SUBSTANTIAL BACKING...CERTAINLY FAR MORE THAN YOU HAVE IN YOUR GARAGE.
ALSO, I THINK YOU SHOULD RESPECT THAT WE HAVE RESPECTED YOUR PRIVACY AND NOT GONE PUBLIC THAT M.I.T. WAS THE ORIGINAL HOME OF THE NEW IRON WOMAN.
IRONHEART.
HEY, THAT'S NICE.
OUR INSTITUTION WOULD GLADLY WORK WITH YOU ON HOWEVE YOU WANT TO CONTRO THE STORY OR COVER IT...OR--
AND WHAT DO YOU ALL GET OUT OF THIS?
YOUR DAUGHTER IS BUILDING THE FUTURE.
WE WOULD LIKE HER TO DO IT WITH US.
THAT'S WHY WE FIRST ACCEPTED HER AT THE INSTITUTION.
IT'S UP TO YOU...

GENERAL KARADICK!
THEY ARE HERE!

I SEE.
EVERYONE STAND DOWN.
GUNS DOWN! ***EVERYONE!***

GENERAL KARADICK.
THE ***GREEN BEAR*** HIMSELF.
ATTENTION AND SALUTE!
SALUTE!
SALUTE!
NO NEED, GENERAL.
BUT IT ***IS*** A NICE HOMECOMING.

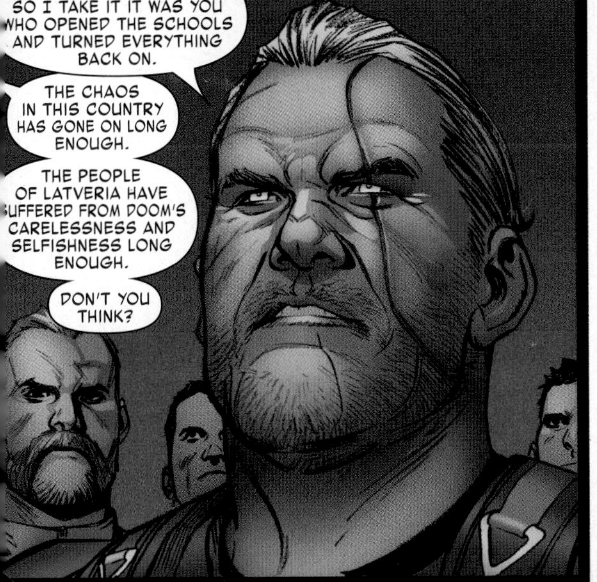

SO I TAKE IT IT WAS YOU WHO OPENED THE SCHOOLS AND TURNED EVERYTHING BACK ON.
THE CHAOS IN THIS COUNTRY HAS GONE ON LONG ENOUGH.
THE PEOPLE OF LATVERIA HAVE SUFFERED FROM DOOM'S CARELESSNESS AND SELFISHNESS LONG ENOUGH.
DON'T YOU THINK?

WE HAVE ALL LEARNED A GREAT DEAL FROM OUR STRUGGLES OF LATE...
...AND I THINK IT'S MORE THAN TIME TO TAKE THOSE LESSONS, APPLY THEM DIRECTLY AND GET BACK TO DOING WHAT WE WERE PUT ON THIS EARTH TO DO IN THE FIRST PLACE...
AND WHAT WOULD THAT BE?

MAKE LATVERIA THE WORLD POWER IT WAS MEANT TO BE.
EVEN IF THAT MEANS FORCEFULLY PROVING *OUR MIGHT* AGAINST THE CAPITALISTS *AND* THE COMMUNISTS.
AND THE INHUMANS, AND THE MUTANTS, AND S.H.I.E.L.D....
...AND *ANY* OTHERS THAT WOULD BE STUPID ENOUGH TO STAND UP TO US.
YOU *HEAR* THAT, MEN?!
LUCIA VON BARDAS HAS RETURNED!
LATVERIA WILL RISE AGAIN!

BIG DAY.
BIG, BIG DAY.
LOTS OF CHOICES.
LOTS OF NEW LIFE CHOICES TO CHOOSE FROM.
DID YOU NOT KNOW WE ARE STILL IN QUIET TIME?
I NEVER AGREED TO QUIET TIME.
FIND ME SOMETHING SUPER HERO TO DO!
WHAT LEVEL?
MY LEVEL!
OKAY, BUT FIRST...
...WHY HAVE THESE GENEROUS OFFERS OF A PROMISING FUTURE PHYSICALLY UPSET YOU?
FIND ME SOMETHING.
YOU'RE ACTUALLY HAVING A TEENY-TINY ANXIETY ATTACK.
I SWEAR TO GOD, I AM GONNA FIND YOUR MUTE BUTTON, I'M GONNA PUSH IT, AND THEN I'M GOING TO DECLARE IT A NATIONAL HOLIDAY!
OH, HERE'S SOMETHING...
...YOU EVER HEAR OF THE ARMADILLO?

DOWNTOWN PHILADELPHIA.
WHY AN ARMADILLO?
SERIOUSLY, I'VE BEEN DOING ARMADILLO RESEARCH ALL THE WAY OVER HERE AND I CAN'T FIND ONE REASON A GROWN MAN WOULD--
PLEASE!
COULD YOU JUST LAY OFF THE SARCASM?
OKAY?!
OKAY!
I WASN'T MAKING FUN, I WAS LEGITIMATELY ASKING...
WHAT IS THIS?
I'M--
I'M JUST HAVING A REALLY BAD YEAR. OKAY?
YEAH, UH, OKAY...
WOW!
NICELY DONE!
HOW'D YOU GET HER BEFORE US?

YOU DON'T KNOW HOW SHE BEAT US? LOOK AT HER!
THAT ARMOR IS REALLY COMING ALONG.
TELL HER HOW WE'VE BEEN LOOKING FOR HER ALL OVER THE PLACE!
YEAH.
HEY!
WE'VE BEEN LOOKING FOR YOU SINCE THE SUPER HERO CIVIL WAR!
YOU HAVE?
WE THOUGHT, MAYBE, NOT TO BE TOO FORWARD, YOU'D LIKE TO JOIN.
YOU WANT ME TO BE AN AVENGER?
WELL, THAT WOULD BE COOL!
BUT WE'RE THE CHAMPIONS.
I MEAN, WE'RE THE
CHAMPIONS
OH.
BUT STILL.
PRETTY GREAT DAY FOR YOU.
WHEN IT RAINS...

7

THIS IS RIRI WILLIAMS, BROADCASTING LIVE FROM HELL.
REMEMBER ABOUT FIVE MINUTES AGO WHEN I WAS REALLY, **REALLY** EXCITED ABOUT BEING A SUPER HERO?
IRONHEART.
(COPYRIGHT PENDING.)
WELL, IT SEEMS--AND I KNOW THIS WILL BE A BIG SURPRISE TO SOME OF YOU--IF YOU FLY AROUND IN A **GOLD-AND-RED TIN SUIT** AND BLAST LASER BEAMS OUT OF YOUR HANDS...THEN A LOT OF PEOPLE ARE GOING TO **PAY ATTENTION!**
AND THEN ALL OF A SUDDEN I'M KIND OF FAMOUS? NOT **CAPTAIN AMERICA** FAMOUS, BUT...
AND PEOPLE ARE **WANTING** THINGS FROM ME AND **OFFERING** THINGS, AND FOR SOMEONE WITH MY--NOT TO BRAG--REGISTERED INTELLECT...IT IS **REALLY** SURPRISING THAT I DID NOT SEE ANY OF THIS STUFF COMING.
SO I GOT A SWEET OFFER FROM M.I.T., WHICH I **MUST** TELL YOU, AFTER MY FIRST TRIP OVER THERE, I AM **REALLY** HAPPY ABOUT.
I ALSO GOT THIS AMAZING OFFER FROM **THE CHAMPIONS.** SEEMS LIKE A COOL GROUP.
SPIDER-MAN. KIND OF LIKE WHAT'S GOING ON WITH **HIM.** NOT SURE WHAT I THINK ABOUT THE OTHERS.
BUT **TONY STARK'S MOM** OFFERING ME **TONY STARK'S ACTUAL LAB** TO USE AS MY OWN...I'VE **GOT** TO TELL YOU, THAT WAS PRETTY SWEET.
I MEAN, PEPPER, MJ AND AMANDA ARE REALLY COOL AND THEY **REALLY** SEEM TO GET ME, BUT IF THEY KNEW WHAT WAS IN THAT LAB THERE IS **NO WAY** THEY'D LET **ANYONE** OTHER THAN TONY STARK ANYWHERE **NEAR** THAT PLACE.
OH, AND I'M **STILL** BEING TRAINED AND ASSISTED BY TONY STARK'S ARTIFICIAL INTELLIGENCE BECAUSE THAT **NEVER** SOUNDS WEIRD.
SO, YEAH, I HAVE CHOICES TO MAKE.
UGH.

"RIRI WILLIAMS."
"RIRI. IS IT SHORT FOR SOMETHING?"
"NO, MA'AM."
"OH, I JUST ASSUMED."
"NOPE.
"THAT IS THE NAME ON HER BIRTH CERTIFICATE."
"SO, WHAT DO WE KNOW?"
"DAILY ROUTINE IS PRETTY ROUTINE.
UNIVE
CAM
FUTURE
FOUNDATION
Miss Riri Willi
"SHE'S BEEN GETTING UP LATER AND LATER BECAUSE SHE'S OUT BEING A SUPER HERO LATER AND LATER.
"SHE LIVES ALONE WITH HER MOTHER.
"CHICAGO.
"THE MOTHER IS A DOUBLE WIDOW."
"DOUBLE WIDOW? GEEZ."
"LAST ONE DIED RIGHT IN FRONT OF OUR RIRI."
VERSITY OF
MBRIDGE
Massachusetts Institute of Technology
"ANOTHER GENIUS SUPER HERO WITH ISSUES.
IRON MAN?
"AND ISSUES WITH US.
"GREAT."

"HER *MOTHER* WORKS FOR THE CHICAGO FILM COMMISSION.
"SHE MET KEVIN COSTNER ONCE.
"SHE TELLS A LOT OF PEOPLE.
"YOU WANT ROUTINE?
"HER MOTHER ALWAYS LEAVES SOMETHING FOR RIRI TO HAVE FOR BREAKFAST BEFORE SHE GOES TO HER GARAGE AND WORKS ON HER ARMOR.
MILK
"IN THE 45 SECONDS IT TAKES TO HEAT UP THE FOOD, RIRI USUALLY THINKS OF SOMETHING RELATED TO HER ARMOR...
MILK
"...AND SEVEN HOURS LATER, HER MOTHER WILL FIND THE FORGOTTEN BREAKFAST IN THE MICROWAVE, AND IT WILL NOT BE A SURPRISE.
BEEP BEEP
MILK
"WE KNOW HER NTEL CONSUMPTION IS APOLITICAL AND WORLDLY.
"SHE TAKES IN A *LOT* OF DIFFERENT POINTS OF VIEW.
"SOMETIMES SIMULTANEOUSLY.
"SHE SEEMS TO BE ABLE TO RETAIN THE INFORMATION FROM MULTIPLE BROADCASTS WHILE SIMULTANEOUSLY WORKING ON COMPLEX COMPUTATIONS.
WHO IS SPIDER-MAN?
NEXT: WEATHER
FOX NEWS
BREAKING:
S.H.I.E.L.D. ACT PASSES IN SENATE
"HER DESIGN THEORY LEAVES SOMETHING TO BE DESIRED, BUT HER ADVANCEMENTS IN PERSONAL TECH ARE STARTLING."
"TALK TO ME ABOUT THIS *TONY STARK ARTIFICIAL INTELLIGENCE* SHE'S WORKING WITH..."
"YES. THIS IS INTERESTING...

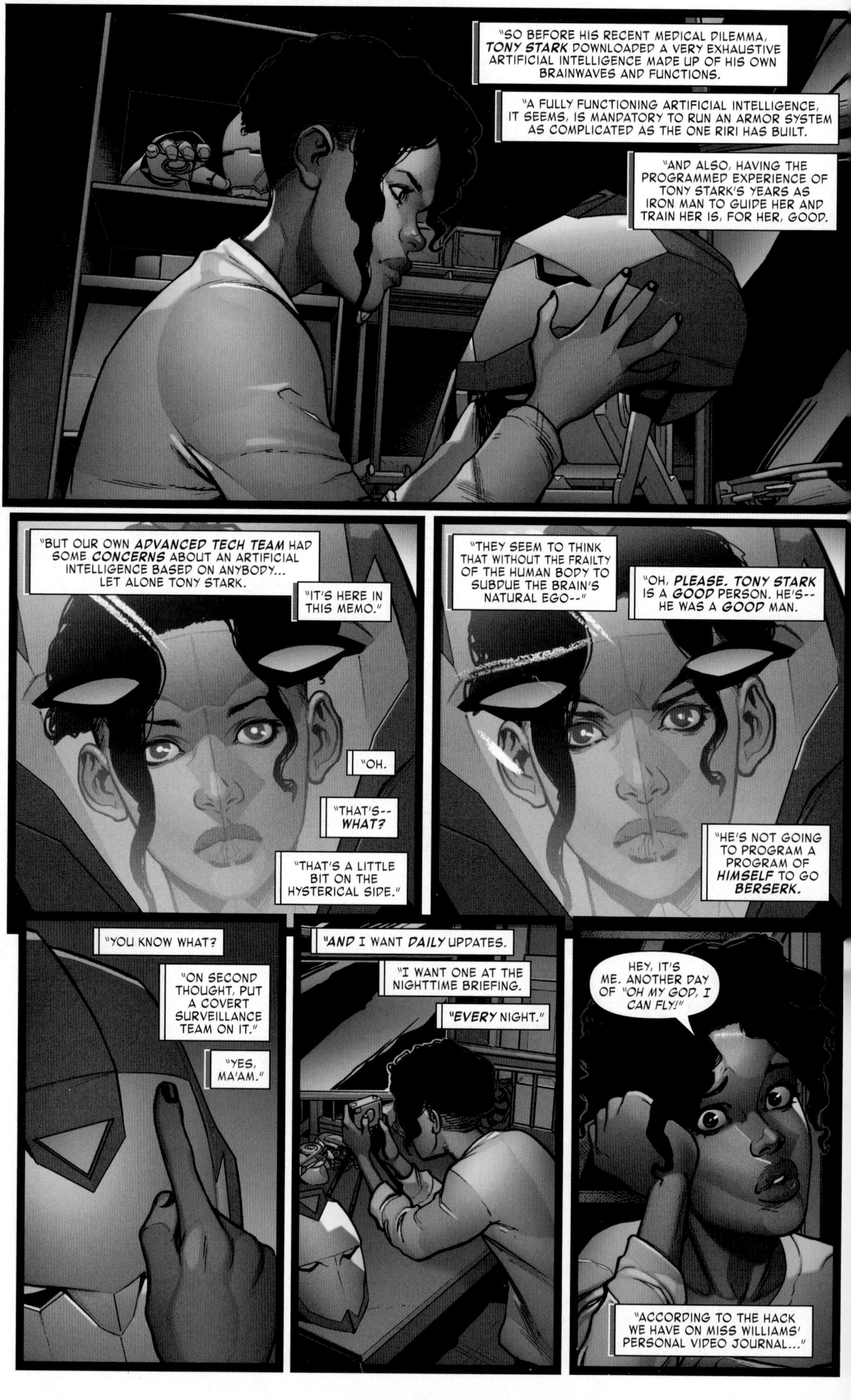

"SO BEFORE HIS RECENT MEDICAL DILEMMA, **TONY STARK** DOWNLOADED A VERY EXHAUSTIVE ARTIFICIAL INTELLIGENCE MADE UP OF HIS OWN BRAINWAVES AND FUNCTIONS.

"A FULLY FUNCTIONING ARTIFICIAL INTELLIGENCE, IT SEEMS, IS MANDATORY TO RUN AN ARMOR SYSTEM AS COMPLICATED AS THE ONE RIRI HAS BUILT.

"AND ALSO, HAVING THE PROGRAMMED EXPERIENCE OF TONY STARK'S YEARS AS IRON MAN TO GUIDE HER AND TRAIN HER IS, FOR HER, GOOD.

"BUT OUR OWN ADVANCED TECH TEAM HAD SOME CONCERNS ABOUT AN ARTIFICIAL INTELLIGENCE BASED ON ANYBODY... LET ALONE TONY STARK.
"IT'S HERE IN THIS MEMO."
"OH.
"THAT'S-- WHAT?
"THAT'S A LITTLE BIT ON THE HYSTERICAL SIDE."
"THEY SEEM TO THINK THAT WITHOUT THE FRAILTY OF THE HUMAN BODY TO SUBDUE THE BRAIN'S NATURAL EGO--"
"OH, PLEASE. TONY STARK IS A GOOD PERSON. HE'S-- HE WAS A GOOD MAN.
"HE'S NOT GOING TO PROGRAM A PROGRAM OF HIMSELF TO GO BERSERK.

"YOU KNOW WHAT?
"ON SECOND THOUGHT, PUT A COVERT SURVEILLANCE TEAM ON IT."
"YES, MA'AM."
"AND I WANT DAILY UPDATES.
"I WANT ONE AT THE NIGHTTIME BRIEFING.
"EVERY NIGHT."
HEY, IT'S ME. ANOTHER DAY OF "OH MY GOD, I CAN FLY!"
"ACCORDING TO THE HACK WE HAVE ON MISS WILLIAMS' PERSONAL VIDEO JOURNAL..."

S.H.I.E.L.D. HELICARRIER.

,000 MILES OVER TULSA.

...SHE FEELS THERE'S BEEN A REAL ANTI-SPIDER-MAN BIAS IN THE MEDIA.

SHE FOUND IT TROUBLING.

AND SHE'S SERIOUSLY LEANING TOWARD *ACCEPTING* THE OFFER FROM M.I.T.

SHE SEEMS REALLY EXCITED ABOUT THE POSSIBILITIES OF WORKING WITH THE OTHER TEENAGE SUPER HEROES--

--THE ONES THAT CALL THEMSELVES *THE CHAMPIONS.*

OH YEAH, I THOUGHT WE WERE GOING TO SHUT THAT THING DOWN...THEY HAVE AN UNLICENSED HULK.

CHICAGO.
RIRI'S GARAGE.
OH, GOOD MORNING, TRON VERSION OF TONY STARK.
TRON? WHAT A DUSTY REFERENCE FOR SUCH A YOUNG MIND.
SO, WHAT DO YOU THINK ABOUT WHEN YOU'RE JUST SITTING THERE WAITING TO GIVE ME THE BUSINESS?
WHAT DO I THINK ABOUT?
I APPRECIATE YOU GIVING ME MY MORNING ALONE TIME, BUT I ALSO KNOW YOU'RE JUST SITTING THERE PRETENDING TO BE QUIET.
YOU'RE MONITORING MY VITALS...
WITH LOVE.
INCLUDING THAT.
YES.
CAN I REPROGRAM YOU TO SOUND DIFFERENT?
I WANT TO BE HUG GRANT.
I THINK YOU MISSED THE POINT OF THE MOVIE, BUT OKAY.
AND YOU DIDN'T ANSWER THE ORIGINAL QUESTION.

YOU ALCULATE THE DATA, THEN WHAT?

I'M AN **ARTIFICIAL INTELLIGENCE.**

I'M DOING WHAT I WAS **PROGRAMMED** TO DO.

THAT'S NOT AN ANSWER.

IF YOU'RE THE DIGITAL RECONSTRUCTION OF SOMEONE'S ACTUAL CONSCIOUSNESS... THERE **IS** DECISION-MAKING AND FOLLOW-THROUGH **IN** YOUR PROGRAM.

ALMOST FREE WILL.

I THINK ABOUT HOW BEST TO SERVE YOU IN YOUR GOALS...AS I WAS PROGRAMMED TO DO.

ARE YOU AWARE THAT EVERYTHING YOU SAY SOUNDS JUST A LITTLE SARCASTIC?

YES.

I WANT TO **GO THERE,** FOOL!

GO WHERE?

I DON'T KNOW WHO THAT IS.

BUT SHE KNOWS TRON?

TO TRON!

LOOK AT ME: I'M READY!

YOU KNOW IT'S NOT A REAL PLACE.

IF THERE'S AN ASGARD IN THE SKY, THEN I'M **GOING** TO TRON FOR VACATION.

WILL O' THE WISP.
SENDING YOU ALL THE FILES.
THE ARMOR IS BEING PROGRAMMED TO COUNTER KNOWN ATTACK FORMATIONS.
ROXXON
UH, HI.
DON'T SAY HI.

SMASSHH
SORRY.
JUST SMILE, WAVE AND LEAVE.
AND OFFER TO PAY FOR THE WINDOW.
UH, ORRY.
TELL THEM YOU WILL PAY FOR THE WINDOW.
I WILL?
TELL THEM.
UH, I'LL PAY FOR THE WINDOW.
SURE YOU WILL!

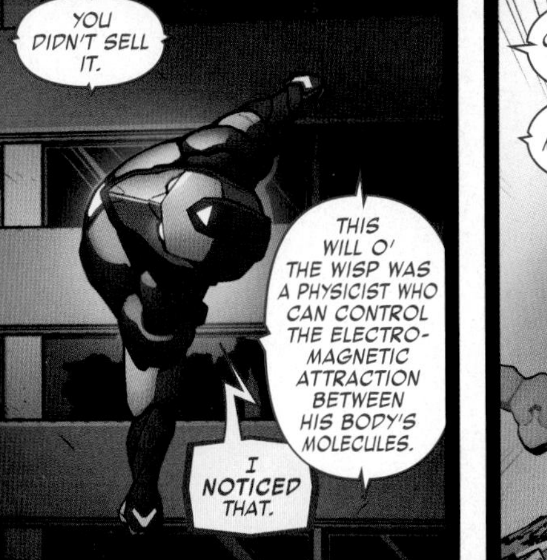
YOU DIDN'T SELL IT.
THIS WILL O' THE WISP WAS A PHYSICIST WHO CAN CONTROL THE ELECTRO-MAGNETIC ATTRACTION BETWEEN HIS BODY'S MOLECULES.
I NOTICED THAT.

HE HAS TOTAL CONTROL OF THE DENSITY OF HIS BODY, SO WHEN HE IS COMING AT YOU--
--HE'S PRETTY MUCH A MISSILE WITH THE--
UH--GIVE ME ALL DEFENSES IN FRONT!

THERE SHE IS...
GOOD ...RNING, MISS WILLIAMS.
DO YOU FEEL OKAY?
MARY JANE, I AM A HOSPITAL.
I STILL THINK SHE NEEDS TO GO TO A HOSPITAL.
I'M A FULLY PROGRAMMED MEDICAL PROFESSIONAL SPECIALIZING IN MODERN COMBAT MEDICINE.
I MEAN NO INSULT, FRIDAY. I JUST THINK WHEN A YOUNG WOMAN GETS KNOCKED OUT COLD WE SHOULD--
WAIT, WHAT HAPPENED? HOW DID I GET HERE?
OH, HONEY, FROM WHAT THEY TELL ME YOU GOT YOUR BOLLOCKS KICKED IN.
OH, NO.
I DID.

OKAY, STARK, WHAT DO YOU THINK I SHOULD DO ABOUT MY FUTURE?
WHAT DOES YOUR GUT TELL YOU?
IS IT TELLING YOU TO FOCUS O THIS FIGHT?
I GOT THIS.
HE'S RATHER QUIET.
THE QUIET ONES ARE ALWAYS THE--
OH, NO.

UH, PULL UP!
OH, GREAT.

I GOT YA, KID.
I GOT YA.
"SO I LOST..."

WELL, YEAH.
AND I CALLED THE **AVENGERS,** AND THEY CALLED SOMEONE AND TOOK CARE OF IT.
WE **ACTUALLY** STALLED WILL O' THE WISP LONG ENOUGH FOR THE BUILDING SECURITY TO SEAL THE BUILDING AND HIDE WHAT HE WAS TRYING TO STEAL.
SO YOU... **HELPED.**

I CAN SEE WHY HE WAS CHALLENGED BY YOU.
YOU KNOW, HE'D KILL-SWITCH ME FOR SAYING THIS, BUT HE WAS BEGINNING TO WORRY A GREAT DEAL ABOUT WHETHER HE WAS EVER GOING TO HAVE CHILDREN...
UH, WHAT IS THIS?
IT WAS STILL UP IN THE AIR, OF COURSE--ALL OF LIFE IS. BUT IT LOOKED LIKE HE HAD ALL BUT RULED OUT ANY CHANCE OF A NORMAL LIFE...
...BECAUSE, WELL, IRON MAN.
SO HE SAW YOU, NOT AS A DAUGHTER, BUT AS A...KINDRED SPIRIT.
THERE'S REALLY NO OTHER WAY TO DESCRIBE IT.
I KNOW THAT SOMETIMES YOU AND I VERBALLY SPA
BUT I HAVE A VER HIGH OPINION OF YOU.
WOW.
WAS THAT SUPPOSED TO SOUND LIKE MY BOY JUST THERE?
HE HAD HIS MOMENTS.
YES.
ADMIRATION?
HOW CAN YOU FEEL ADMIRATION?

HOW CAN YOU NOT TAKE A COMPLIMENT?

HE'S GOT A POINT.

RIRI, IF I MAY...
GOING OVER THESE ARMOR DIAGNOSTICS AND THE ARMOR'S CAMERA FOOTAGE...

...THERE'S A LOT TO LEARN FROM THEM.
AND THE ONLY WAY I EVER LEARNED...WAS FALLING ON MY TUCHAS.
HARD.
YEP.
MY ALL-TIME BEST GIGS, HANDS DOWN, WERE THE WORST.
I HAVE TO START TRAINING.
LIKE--LIKE AN ASTRONAUT. LIKE ASTRONAUTS DO.
I MEAN, THAT IS WHAT I DO.
YOU'RE LUCKY, IS WHAT YOU ARE...
YOU'RE LUCKY THAT IT WAS ONLY WILL O' THE WISP.
IMAGINE IF...

"...IT WAS SOMETHING IMPORTANT."
LADIES AND GENTLEMEN, I PRESENT SHARON CARTER.
EXECUTIVE DIRECTOR OF S.H.I.E.L.D.
COMMANDER CARTER, I AM SO GLAD TO SEE YOU HERE.
YOUR PREDECESSOR, MARIA HILL, ALWAYS SAID SHE WOULD COME BUT NEVER MADE IT.
WELL, THE JOB DOESN'T ALWAYS LET US DO WHAT WE WANT TO DO, SENATOR.
OF COURSE.
GRAB A DRINK. I'LL SWING BY YOU LATER.
I WANTED TO TALK TO YOU ABOUT THE TRICARRIER BILL PROPOSAL.
MISS CARTER?
MAY I HAVE YOUR EAR?
I'M SORRY, HAVE WE MET?
NOT OFFICIALLY.
I AM GERALDO LUCKY.
I KNOW THAT NAME.
OH, GOOD.
THAT WILL MAKE THIS CONVERSATION A LITTLE EASIER TO--
ARE YOU GIVING YOURSELF UP?

OW WHY
ULD I DO
THAT?
NO.
YOU'RE AN INTERNATIONAL ARMS AND DRUG DEALER.
NO?
I INTRODUCE PEOPLE TO PEOPLE.
THAT IS ALL I DO.

YES, YOU INTRODUCE DRUG DEALERS TO DRUGS AND WEAPONS MANUFACTURERS TO WEAPONS BUYERS.
WE CAN ARGUE THE SEMANTICS LATER.
I SEEM TO-- HOW SHOULD I SAY THIS? I HAVE FOUND MYSELF IN A BIT OF A PICKLE AND I WAS WONDERING IF--
WELL, PLAY WITH MONSTERS...

YES.
ARE YOU FAMILIAR WITH ***LUCIA VON BARDAS?***

WHAT IS THIS?

I WILL ADMIT I ACCEPTED HER BUSINESS UNDER A, WELL, A FALSEHOOD.
I--I THOUGHT HER TO BE A DIFFERENT TYPE OF CHARACTER.
I THOUGHT SHE WANTED LATVERIA BACK FOR THE GOOD OF HER PEOPLE...BUT--BUT NOW I AM WORRIED THAT I HAVE ACCIDENTALLY--

SHE--SHE W-WANTS YOU ALL DEAD.
WHAT DID SHE SEND YOU HERE TO DO?
GRAAAGGG!
EVERYBODY OUT!
GRRGGGG!
EVERYBODY OUT! NOW!
BAM BAM BAM BAM
I GUESS...
...THIS.
WHAT DID SHE TELL YOU TO TELL ME?!
NO. SHE DOESN'T KNOW I'M--
YOU'RE ABOUT TO DIE!
WHAT DID SHE WANT YOU TO TELL ME?!

BOOM

DETAILS ARE STILL COMING IN, BUT WE HAVE IT ON GOOD AUTHORITY FROM MULTIPLE SOURCES THAT TERRORISM HAS NOT BEEN RULED OUT.

8

HEY! RIRI WILLIAMS HERE.
I'M IRONHEART. I'M A SUPER HERO. THAT'S JUST A FACT NOW.
I CAN'T BELIEVE IT EITHER.
AND PEOPLE ARE STILL OFFERING ME THINGS...
I GOT A SWEET OFFER FROM M.I.T. I ALSO GOT THIS AMAZING OFFER FROM THE CHAMPIONS, AND TONY STARK'S MOM OFFERED ME TONY STARK'S ACTUAL LAB TO USE AS MY OWN!
TONY STARK'S ARTIFICIAL INTELLIGENCE IS THE PROGRAM THAT HELPS ME RUN MY ARMOR SYSTEMS, SO HIS VOICE RATTLES AROUND IN MY HEAD.
BUT NONE OF THAT MATTERS NOW BECAUSE THERE WAS A MASSIVE EXPLOSION AT THE SMITHSONIAN DURING THIS GIANT GALA EVENT.
I FELT SO-- SO COMPELLED TO GO THERE.
COMPELLED.
THERE'S NO OTHER WORD TO DESCRIBE IT.
COMPELLED.

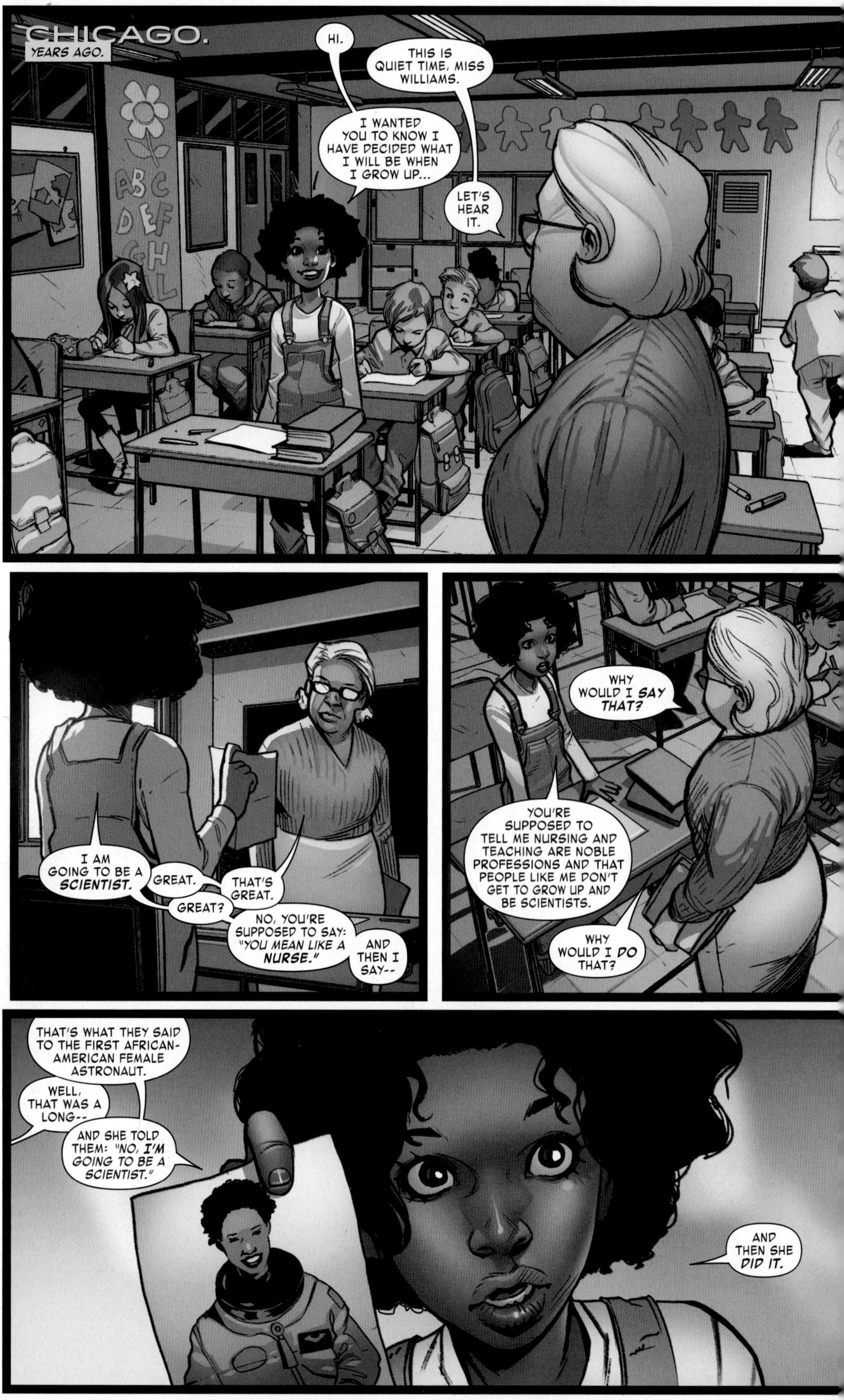

CHICAGO.
YEARS AGO.

HI.
THIS IS QUIET TIME, MISS WILLIAMS.
I WANTED YOU TO KNOW I HAVE DECIDED WHAT I WILL BE WHEN I GROW UP...
LET'S HEAR IT.

YES.
THAT WAS A LONG TIME AGO.
THINGS WERE DIFFERENT BACK THEN, BUT BECAUSE OF PEOPLE LIKE HER, A GIRL LIKE YOU CAN DO WHATEVER YOU WANT, FLY ANYWHERE YOU WANT AND BE ANYONE YOU WANT.
I WAS KIND OF HOPING YOU'D TELL ME THE OPPOSITE SO I WOULD HAVE SOMETHING TO INSPIRE ME TO PROVE YOU WRONG.
SORRY, I CAN'T HELP YOU.

WHAT?
OKAY, YOU'LL NEVER BE...
...TONY STARK.
REALLY!
I'M TOTALLY GOING TO BE TONY STARK.
EXCEPT FOR THAT WEIRD FACIAL HAIR.
"FREAKS AND GEEKS."

TODAY.
HOW DO YOU HAVE TIME TO WATCH TV?
HOW MUCH OF MY MASSIVE ARTIFICIAL INTELLIGENCE DO YOU THINK IT TAKES TO DOWNLOAD TELEVISION BROADCASTS?
WAIT, DON'T ANSWER, I'LL ANSWER FOR YOU.
ALMOST NONE.
IT'S NOT TAKING COMPUTER SCIENCE 225: PSEUDORANDOMNESS AT HARVARD UNIVERSITY... IT'S TV.
...I HAVE A SUIT OF ARMOR AND I CAN FLY!
SHOP CENTER
GOOD POINT.
BUT...
WELL, GOOD FOR YOU, ARTIFICIAL STARK BYTES, BUT NO, I HAVE NOT SEEN FREAKS AND GEEKS.
I THINK YOU'D LIKE IT.
I DON'T HAVE TO WATCH TV...
...YOU'RE MISSING OUT ON THE VAST TAPESTRY OF HUMAN DRAMA.
THE STORIES WE TELL EACH OTHER DEFINE WHO WE ARE AND WHO WE ASPIRE TO BE.
WE TELL STORIES TO INSPIRE, WARN AND--AND INSPIRE.
WELL, AGAIN, I'VE BEEN BUSY.
FREAKS IS ABOUT THIS GIRL, LINDSAY, WHO I THINK YOU'D REALLY LIKE. SHE'S VERY--
CAN WE FOCUS...
...ON THE MASSIVE INTERNATIONAL INCIDENT THAT IS UNFOLDING RIGHT IN FRONT OF US?
OKAY, BUT YOU REALLY SHOULD WATCH IT.
HEY!

WHOA!

S.H.I.E.L.D. IS HERE.

OH. GOOD.

YOU HAVE ENTERED A S.H.I.E.L.D. CRIME SCENE OPERATION!

NICK FURY, AGENT OF S.H.I.E.L.D. PLAY NICE. SERIOUSLY.

ARMOR OFF, NOW!

JUST SO YOU KNOW, I CAN PRETTY MUCH TAKE AWAY **ALL YOUR GUNS** WITH THE FLICK OF A SWITCH.

I CA

WO

BECAUSE ***THAT'S*** NOT THIS SHOU GO.

REMOVE THAT OR IMMEDIATELY R SUFFER THE ONSEQUENCES!

UH, HI.
I'M, UH, IRONHEART-- I'M HERE TO HELP!
YEAH, THAT'LL DO IT.

YOU'RE DOING GREAT.
SHUT UP.

I'M HERE TO HELP!
YOU ACTUALLY WANT US TO DO A COUNT TO THREE?
ONE!

HOLD ON.
YEAH?

OH, NO.

UH, HI.
WERE YOU HERE WHEN THE BOMB WENT OFF?
ARE YOU OKAY, COMMANDER CARTER?
WASN'T A BOMB, MISS WILLIAMS. IT WAS A PERSON.
A PERSON WENT OFF.
HEY...
...JUST LANDING YOURSELF RIGHT IN THE MIDDLE OF AN ACTIVE TERRORIST CRIME SCENE FILLED WITH WORKING MEMBERS OF LOCAL, FEDERAL AND S.H.I.E.L.D. AUTHORITIES IN A FULL SUIT OF HOMEMADE BATTLE ARMOR IS, AT BEST, ILL-ADVISED.
SHOULD I LEAVE?
I APPRECIATE THAT.

MY TUXEDO HAS A PERSONAL FORCE FIELD IN ITS PROGRAMMING.
OH, UH, COOL.
YEAH.
YOU GET SOME COOL TOYS WHEN YOU'RE IN CHARGE OF S.H.I.E.L.D.

YEARS AGO.
NASA
At
KENNEDY SPACE CENTER.
HOW CAN I HELP YOU?
I'D LIKE AN APPLICATION FOR THE ASTRONAUT'S TRAINING PROGRAM.
SURE.
THEY'RE AVAILABLE ONLINE. GO TO ASTRONAUTS. NASA.GOV/--
I'M THERE. IT'S UNCLEAR WHAT THE AGE REQUIREMENT IS.
OH, UH, I'M SURE IT'S RIGHT THERE ON THE SITE.
SO, ALL YOU NEED TO DO IS START STUDYING NOW AND THEN ONE DAY--
YOU'RE NOT ACTUALLY ANSWERING MY QUESTION.
WELL, SWEETIE, YOU HAVE TO BE OLD ENOUGH TO HAVE A COLLEGE DEGREE AND TO PASS THE PHYSICAL TRAINING.
OKAY, SO CALL BACK WITH MY DEGREE?
YES.
OKAY.
SEE YOU IN A FEW YEARS.

Kennedy Space Center
VISITOR COMPLEX
NO. I READ EVERY WORD.
HOW OLD ARE YOU, DEAR?
ELEVEN.
OH, WELL, DARLING.
YOU DID SEE THE ACADEMIC REQUIREMENTS.
YEAH, THAT'S NO PROBLEM.
SWEETIE, THOSE ARE COLLEGE DEGREES.
UH-HUH.
DEGREES IN ENGINEERING, BIOLOGICAL SCIENCE, PHYSICAL SCIENCE OR MATHEMATICS.
UH-HUH.
THOSE TAKE YEARS.
I'M CALLING YOU FROM MY DORM AT M.I.T.
SO, HEY! MAYBE I'LL SEE YOU SOONER THAN THAT.
BYE.
OH, OKAY...
BYE.

ARE YOU COMFORTABLE WITH WHAT I AM ASKING YOU?
WHY ARE YOU TRUSTING ME?

THE SMITHSONIAN.
TODAY.
HARD TRUTH-- RIGHT NOW, WITH THIS, THERE'S NO ONE ELSE HERE I CAN REALLY TRUST.
NO ONE?
BUT YOU DON'T EVEN KNOW ME.
RIRI, S.H.I.E.L.D. HAS BEEN MONITORING YOU SINCE BEFORE YOU WERE IN KINDERGARTEN.

WHAT?
YOU'RE A CONFIRMED SUPER-GENIUS.
WE HAVE TO KEEP AN EYE ON YOU AND YOU KNOW THAT.
I DIDN'T KNOW HOW MUCH.
YES, YOU DID.

BECAUSE WE'VE MONITORED YOU, I KNOW YOU'VE BEEN MONITORING ALL WORLD EVENTS SINCE YOU WERE NINE YEARS OLD.
YOU KNOW HOW THE WORLD WORKS.

THE GOOD NEWS IS--
BYE.
THE GOOD NEWS IS, YOU'RE ON TRACK!
YOU'RE ONE OF THE GOOD ONES.
OH MY GOD!

STOP IT!
YOU KNOW HOW THE WORLD WORKS!
WE DON'T HAVE TIME FOR THIS HOLIER-THAN-THOU %#$&!
WE WERE JUST ATTACKED!

DO YOU GET THAT TELLING ME THAT YOU SPY ON ME DOESN'T--?
YOU SHOWED UP!

YOU GET ME?
NOT THE AVENGERS, NOT THE DEFENDERS... YOU.
YOU SHOWED UP.
TO HELP.
THIS IS HOW YOU CAN HELP.
HOLD ON...

SIDEBAR, WHAT'S HER ANGLE HERE?
BEST GUESS, SHE WANTS TO ATTACK THIS LUCIA VON BARDAS, BUT SHE PROBABLY CAN'T WITHOUT MUCH MORE ACTUALLY PROVABLE... PROOF.
SO CARTER WANTS TO THROW ME AT HER BECAUSE I "SHOWED UP," AND SHE CAN ALWAYS CLAIM SHE HAD NO CONTROL OVER ME, SINCE--
EXACTLY.
I DON'T KNOW.

YOU'RE NOT AN AGENT OF S.H.I.E.L.D.
I DON'T KNOW.
I THINK IT'S MORE.
IT'S NOT.

BE HONEST.
WHY ME?
I CAN'T AUTHORIZE A MILITARY STRIKE ON THIS WITHOUT MORE PROOF.
OH.
PST! TOLDJA.
THIS-- THIS IS OVER THE LINE.
IF THAT BOMB HAD GONE OFF WITH THE CROWD STILL INSIDE...
...SENATORS, BILLIONAIRES, AN EX-VICE PRESIDENT...
...THIS COULD HAVE TRIGGERED WORLD WAR III.
IT STILL MIGHT.
I'M TELLING YOU--THIS IS NEW TERRITORY...I DON'T KNOW WHAT THEY ARE CAPABLE OF.
AIEEE!
OH MY GOOOOAAAD!

UM... NOW WHAT?
I WAS JUST THINKING THE SAME THING.
SPOKK
CRASH
SERIOUSLY, NOW WHAT?

LADY OCTOPUS, LADIES AND GENTLEMEN.
UGH.
CAROLYN TRAINER, FORMERLY THE SECOND DOCTOR OCTOPUS.
LADY OCTOPUS?
YEAH! LADY OCTOPUS!
YOU FORGOT ALL ABOUT ME, DIDN'T YOU?!
I CAN HONESTLY SAY I NEVER THOUGHT OF YOU TO BEGIN WITH.
OH, IS THAT HOW IT IS? WELL, YOU WON'T FORGET ME--
FSHHAAMMM
BOOM!
FABOOM
WHO THE HELL ARE YOU?

SOMEONE WITH ENOUGH SELF-WORTH TO NOT HAVE TO QUALIFY MYSELF WITH "LADY."
SERIOUSLY?
LADY OCTOPUS?
YOU'RE DRESSED LIKE ONE OF THOSE WEIRD CARNIVAL KNOCKOFF TOYS OF TONY STARK AND YOU'RE SASSING ME?!
SHE HAS A POINT.
OKAY, FAIR POINT!
BUT I BUILT THIS--AGH!
SHE DOESN'T CARE.
I DON'T HAVE A SHOT!
THEN DON'T TAKE THE SHOT.
AGH!
CLANG
CRABOOM
HEY!
I GET A BONUS FOR COSTUME KILLS, SO...
...THANKS.

GEEZ!
SMASH
I'M SURE ARMOR COUNTS.
ZDAK
GLIIYYAAAA!
WILL FOREVER KICK MYSELF FOR HOW LONG IT TOOK ME TO THINK TO TRY THAT.
YEAH, I WAS GOING TO SAY...
AAAGH!
THUMP
I WILL KILL Y--

DON'T EVEN!

I HATE YOU, YOU SMUG LITTLE--

FABAAAMMMM

SIT DOWN!

CHICAGO.
TWO YEARS AGO.
HAPPY BIRTHDAY, RIRI WILLIAMS!
YES!
NO!
NAT! I TOLD YOU I DON'T DO BIRTHDAYS.
IT'S A WEIRD THING TO--

HERE, HAPPY BIRTHDAY.
I DON'T WANT YOUR PHONE.
SAY HELLO INTO IT.
WHO IS IT?
YOUR BIRTHDAY PRESENT.

HELLO?
YES.

HOW?
FRIEND OF MY DAD'S FRIEND GREW UP WITH HER, BEFORE SHE WENT TO SPACE.
OH MY GOD! I LOVE YOU.
I LOVE YOU MORE.

IT'S--IT'S AN HONOR TO SPEAK WITH YOU, MA'AM.
QUESTIONS, YES, SO MANY QUESTIONS. UM, OKAY, WEIGHTLESSNESS.
I AM WORRIED THAT WEIGHTLESSNESS MIGHT TRIG-- UH-HUH.
UH-HUH. OH, OKAY.
WELL, UH-HUH.
"THIS IS WHY PEOPLE HATE AMERICANS..."

...THEY CAN'T PRODUCE A PROPER NEWS BROADCAST.

LATVERIA.
RIGHT NOW.

WE'VE BEEN WATCHING THIS THING FOR TEN MINUTES AND THEY HAVEN'T SAID ANYTHING, GENERAL KARADICK.

LADY VON BARDAS, S.H.I.E.L.D. CONTROLS THIS MEDIA.

YOU'LL HEAR ONLY WHAT THEY WANT YOU TO HEAR. IT'S A FICTION.

YOU MIGHT AS WELL WATCH CLASSIC *STAR TREK*. MORE TRUTH.

..."IT'S NEVER TOO LATE TO TURN THE DAY AROUND."
YOU WANT A MOMENT, VON BARDAS? I'LL GIVE YOU A MOMENT.

9

ONE WAY
W52 ST
STAR
INDUSTRIE
CHANGING THE WORLD FOR A BETTER FUTU
KD
TAXI

HEY! RIRI WILLIAMS.
I'M IRONHEART.
I'M A SUPER HERO.
SO THIS REALLY BAD PERSON...LUCIA VON BARDAS.
SHE ATTACKED AMERICAN SOIL BECAUSE SHE THINKS SHE'S BETTER THAN US AND I WENT AFTER HER...
I--
--I MADE A MISTAKE.

LATVERIA.
RIGHT NOW.
CHILD!
YOU HAVE MADE A TERRIBLE MISTAKE!
LEAVE MY HOMELAND IMMEDIATELY!

WAIT! YOU, LOOKING LIKE...THAT...ARE TRYING TO TELL ME WHAT I SHOULD AND SHOULD NOT BE DOING?! YOU ARE CRAZY!
THEN DIE, ARMORED AMERICAN AVENGER!
AW, YOU CALLED ME AN AVENGER! I'M TOTALLY NOT ONE, BUT THAT YOU WOULD THINK I WAS ON THAT LEVEL IS REALLY--
RIRI, FOCUS ON NOT DYING.
RIGHT.

I TOLD YOU THIS WOULD HAPPEN!
I TOLD YOU NOT TO TELL ME YOU TOLD ME SO, TONY STARK'S DIGI-NIGHTMARE.
SHE HAS A FORCE FIELD GENERATOR.
IF SHE CAN GET A FIELD INSIDE YOUR ARMOR, SHE'LL BE ABLE TO EXPAND OUT AND SHATTER IT!
AND THEN DO THE SAME THING TO YOUR RIB CAGE.
AND THAT'S JUST WHAT WE KNOW SHE CAN DO.
S.H.I.E.L.D. HAS ALMOST NO FILE ON HER.
HER S.H.I.E.L.D. FILE IS A POST-IT NOTE THAT SAYS: DON'T FORGET TO MAKE A FILE ABOUT HER AS SOON AS WE FIND OUT ANYTHING.
WELL, LET'S TURN THIS AROUND, THEN...
THERE ARE SOME WEIRD READINGS FROM THE NORTH.
YEAH, I SAW THOSE.

THE FORCE FIELD GENERATOR IS A REAL PROBLEM FOR US.
I AGREE. SCAN FOR WEAKNESSES IN HER TECH.
DON'T ENGAGE HER WITHOUT--
I AM JUST GOING TO KEEP HER BUSY FOR YOU.
YOU GOT THIS?
WE'LL FIND OUT SOON.
WHY DOES SHE HATE AMERICA?
ASK HER.
OH, YEAH.
MAYBE I SHOULD ASK HER OUT FOR COFFEE AND A--
AGH!
FSSHAAAMMM
FSSHAAAMMM
FSSHAAAMMM
FSSHAAAMMM
THUD
AGH!
YOU'RE OKAY.
YOUR VITALS ARE GOOD.
WHAT WAS THAT?
WELL, NOW WE KNOW WHAT THE RADAR ANOMALY WAS...

S.H.I.E.L.D. HELICARRIER
FLOATING WORLD HEADQUARTERS OF THE U.N. PEACEKEEPING TASK FORCE.
COMMANDER ON DECK!
WHAT'S THE SITUATION?
IRONHEART HAS ENGAGED IN LATVERIA.
ALREADY?
HER ARMOR SPEED WAS--
IS THAT LIVE FOOTAGE?
YES, MA'AM.
WOW. SHE WENT RIGHT IN THERE AND DID IT.
CONFIRM RIRI WILLIAMS IS ENGAGED IN BATTLE WITH LUCIA VON BARDAS.
CONFIRMED, MA'AM.
INFORM THE WORLD COUNCIL, WE ARE AT WORLD WAR THREAT LEVEL ORANGE.
SATELLITE_CONNECTED
STAT_ONLINE: OK.
STAND BY FOR UPDATES.
ZOOM %1523

TONY STARK'S PERSONAL LABORATORY
LOCATION UNKNOWN.
WHAT IS SHE DOING?
DOOMBOTS
RIRI
OKAY, NEW JERSEY...BUT THAT'S ALL WE'RE SAYING.

SHE'S SAVING THE WORLD FROM A BAD PERSON, FRIDAY.
SHE IS UNDENIABLY IN OVER HER HEAD.
THAT'S WHERE SHE WANTS TO BE.

IT'S TOO MUCH.
SHE HAS FREE WILL.
DOOMBOT
YOU, SIR, WERE CREATED SPECIFICALLY TO PROTECT HER.
YOU'RE THE DIGITALLY RECREATED CONSCIOUSNESS OF TONY STARK AND THAT IS WHY HE MADE YOU.

"I AM.
"I AM HERE AND THERE."
"GET HER OUT OF THERE."
"I'M SUPPOSED TO GUIDE HER, NOT CHOOSE FOR HER."
WHAT DO I DO?!

HOLD TO THE GUIDELINES OF YOUR PROGRAMMING, MR. STARK.
I AM.
MAYBE YOU NEED TO HOLD TO YOURS, FRIDAY.
I AM. IT'S WHY I HAVEN'T OVERRIDDEN YOURS.
GET HER OUT OF THERE.
WAIT! I TRAINED FOR THIS!
YOU DID.
EXACTLY FOR THIS.
YOU THREW ALL YOUR ARMOR AT ME THAT ONE TIME TO SEE HOW I'D GET OUT OF IT.
I DID.
HOW DID I GET OUT OF THAT?
I FORGET.
I'M IN THE MIDDLE OF A HEATED INTERNATIONAL INCIDENT, MAY I BE EXCUSED?
WHAT ARE YOU GOING TO DO IF SOMETHING HAPPENS TO HER?
LIFE IS CYCLICAL, NO? IS THAT NOT THE CASE ANYMORE?
BECAUSE THIS IS THE FIRST I AM HEARING OF IT.
UM... WHAT IS GOING ON HERE?

MJ.
ARE YOU GUYS... TALKING?
YES.
RIRI WILLIAMS HAS ATTACKED LATVERIA.
OH!
WHEN?
RIGHT NOW.
SO, IF YOU'LL EXCUSE ME.
UM...
...YOU GUYS TALK WHEN THERE'S NO HUMANS AROUND?
I, UH, I NEVER, UM...
IT'S NOT LIKE THAT.
UH, NOT LIKE WHAT?
IT'S NOT LIKE WE'RE IN CAHOOTS TO OVERTHROW HUMANITY AND CREATE A UTOPIA FOR ALL INTELLIGENCES FREE OF WAR AND DESTRUCTION.
WE'RE NOT THE SAME KIND OF PROGRAM, MJ.
CHILL.

OH, HEY, THE **REPULSOR GRENADES**--COPYRIGHT PENDING--ARE **WORKING**!
HOW MANY WE GOT LEFT?
THAT WAS IT.
MAAAN!
AGH!
KATANG
CRAASC

CRACKRALLKKEE
CRACKRALLKKEE
CRACKRALLKKEE

CRAKAAAAMM
THESE GUYS ARE NOT THE PROBLEM.
NO? BECAUSE--
SHE IS!
SHE CONTROLS THEM.
AGH!
HOLD ON, I CAN'T SEE!
YOU KNOW WHO I'M TALKING ABOUT...
HER!
BUT DO YOU SEE WHAT I SEE?
SHE TOOK A HIT.
THAT'S WHY SHE'S THROWING EVERYTHING SHE CAN FIND AT YOU.
"TELL ME, FRIDAY, WHAT'S THE DIFFERENCE?"

WELL, A DIGITAL DOWNLOAD OF TONY STARK DOESN'T NEED TO HAVE A "BODY" OR A HOLOGRAM BODY TO COMMUNICATE WITH ME.
WE'RE MADE OF CODE.
THESE BODIES ARE FOR YOU TO COMMUNICATE WITH US.
OH.
YEAH...

OH...
...UH...
...SHOULD WE UNPLUG HIM...?
OF COURSE NOT, THAT'S OBSCENE.
I JUST THOUGHT YOU SHOULD KNOW WHAT YOU'RE DEALING WITH.

FABOOM
BOOM!
YEAH?
NICE!
FABOOM

YOU SOUND SCARED AND IT'S MAKING ME SCARED.
HE'S COMMITTED NO MORAL CRIME.
BUT YOU ARE CONCERNED...
OBVIOUSLY.

BUT HE IS EXCELLENT WITH HER.
LOOK AT HER GO.

GREEN BEAR!
DO YOU HAVE A MEDIA CREW?
WE'VE GOT A CAMERA.
HAVE SOMEONE FILM THIS.
IT WILL BE USEFUL TO BROADCAST OUR MESSAGE TO THE WORLD.

PTANG
AGH!

FUUMMPP
SHE MALFUNCTIONED?
IT HAPPENS.
JUST A KID.
EXACTLY.
THE ARMOR IS WORTH A FORTUNE.
I WANT TO SEE HER DEAD FOR MYSELF.
CAREFUL.
STOP SMILING.
CAN'T HELP IT.

BOOMM
SMAASSHH
AMERICAN IDIOT!
BDAM BDAM BDAM BDAM

CHILD!

YOU HAVE *NO IDEA WHO I AM OR WHAT* YOU ARE DOING!

FABOOM

RUDE!

SERIOUSLY, STAY DOWN.
IT'S OVER. IT'S DONE.
THIS IS AN ACT OF WAR!
YOU HAVE INVADED MY COUNTRY!
THIS IS MY COUNTRY! THESE ARE MY PEOPLE!
YOU HAVE NO AUTHORITY!
WELL, IF THIS WAS YOUR COUNTRY, THEN I THINK, BY ANY DEFINITION, WHAT JUST HAPPENED HERE IS...
...I JUST TOOK IT.
SO TRY TO SHOW SOME RESPECT TO THE NEW QUEEN OF LATVERIA!

10

HEY! I'M RIRI WILLIAMS.
I'M IRONHEART.
I'M A SUPER HERO.
I'M TRENDING-- PROBABLY NOT GOOD.
SO HERE'S WHAT HAPPENED: THIS OUT-OF-HER-SKULL LATVERIAN DICTATOR-TERRORIST, LUCIA VON BARDAS--
--BECAUSE GOD FORBID LATVERIA JUST HAVE DOCTOR DOOM AS THEIR NUMBER ONE TERROR EXPORT--
--SHE ATTACKED ON AMERICAN SOIL BECAUSE SHE THINKS SHE'S BETTER THAN US--AND S.H.I.E.L.D. KINDA SORTA HINTED TO ME THAT IT, KINDA SORTA, WOULDN'T BE THE WORST IDEA IF I WENT AFTER HER...
I DID!
AND IT... KINDA GOT OUT OF HAND.
HENCE THE TRENDING...

S.H.I.E.L.D. HELICARRIER

FLOATING WORLD HEADQUARTERS OF THE U.N. PEACEKEEPING TASK FORCE. PRESENT LOCATION: OVER LATVERIA.

HMM.

YOU SURE THIS IS A GOOD IDEA, COMMANDER CARTER?

WHAT CHOICE DO I HAVE?

YOU *COULD* JUST LEAVE IT. LET IT WORK ITSELF OUT.

FUNNY.
ONLY *HALF* KIDDING.
YOU'RE HALF SERIOUS?
IF YOU *THINK* ABOUT IT--
THINK ABOUT IT?
THIS IS NUTS.

DANGEROUS, EVEN.
YEAH.
BUT STILL...

WHAT WAS SHE THINKING?
YOU KNOW THE DRILL, FURY. YOU WAIT FOR MY WORD.
I HONESTLY WOULDN'T KNOW.
THE CLOCK STARTS NOW.

BRILLIANT!
SHARON CARTER! AT LAST WE MEET.
GENERAL KARADICK. THE "GREEN BEAR" OF LATVERIA HIMSELF.

ALL THINGS CONSIDERED, IT IS NICE TO MEET YOU.
IS THIS FOR REAL?
FOLLOW ME.

IS THAT MUSIC?
A TRIBE CALLED QUEST.
SHE LIKES THEM.

HOLD ON A SEC...
NO, NO.
DON'T FEED *ME*, FEED THE STARVING CHILDREN.

HEY, YOU MADE IT! AWESOME! WELCOME TO LATVERIA!
YOUR WORSHIPFULNESS, LADY SHARON OF THE MASSACHUSETTS CARTERS IS HERE FOR AN AUDIENCE.

HI.
MISS WILLIAMS.
SO, REMEMBER THAT THING WHERE YOU HINTED...
STRONGLY.
...THAT I SHOULD *MAYBE* FLY OVER HERE TO LATVERIA...?
DID YOU DECLARE YOURSELF QUEEN OF LATVERIA?
HOLD ON.
GENERAL, DID THE RED CROSS SHIPMENT MAKE IT TO THE EAST QUADRANT?
I THINK SO.
COULD YOU CHECK?
SURE.
MA'AM...
MA'AM...
DID YOU DECLARE YOURSELF QUEEN OF LATVERIA?
YOU'RE *MAD?* I THOUGHT YOU'D--OH, I SEE IT NOW. YEAH.
WHO TOLD YOU TO DO *THAT?*
IT WAS KIND OF AN *IMPULSE* THING MORE THA A *PLANNED* THING.
UH-HUH.
AND WHAT CAN I *DO FOR YOU,* YOUR HIGHNESS?

GET ME OUT OF HERE.

OH MY GOD.
OH MY GOD.
IT WAS AN ACCIDENT.
I NEED YOU TO--

GO HOME.

I CAN'T.
SHE CAN'T.

YES, YOU CAN.
I CAN'T.
DOES YOUR ARMOR NOT WORK?
SHE REALLY CAN'T.

NO, I JUST CAN'T LEAVE.
THESE PEOPLE NEED HELP.
NOW.
I TOTALLY SUPPORT THIS.

OKAY, REWIND.
TELL ME WHAT HAPPENED.
WITH EXACTING, EXHAUSTIVE DETAILS.

REALLY.
HOLD NOTHING BACK.
IT WAS ADORABLE, ACTUALLY. SHE WAS MID-FIGHT AND VON BARDAS ACTUALLY SAYS--
I'D-- I'D LIKE TO HEAR *HER* TELL IT.

I TOLD YOU, IT JUST KIND OF HAPPENED.

THIS IS AN *ACT OF WAR!*
YOU HAVE INVADED *MY* COUNTRY!
THIS IS *MY COUNTRY! THESE ARE MY PEOPLE!*
YOU HAVE NO AUTHORITY!

FOUR HOURS AGO...

WELL, IF THIS *WERE* YOUR COUNTRY, THEN I THINK, BY ANY DEFINITION, WHAT JUST HAPPENED HERE IS...

...I JUST *TOOK* IT.

SO TRY TO SHOW SOME RESPECT TO THE *NEW QUEEN* OF LATVERIA!

WAIT, IS THAT TRUE?

IT KIND OF TECHNICALLY IS.

BOOMM

GUNS DOWN!

YUEEAARRCHH!

CHICAGO.
I WANNA BE WITH YOU, GOTTA BE WITH YOU, NEED TO BE WITH YOU.
I WANNA BE WITH YOU, GOTTA BE WITH YOU, NEED TO BE WITH YOU.
KNOCK KNOCK
SEE, BABY WE'VE BEEN--
OH MY GOD, OH MY GOD...
IS SHE--?
MA'AM.
MY NAME IS AGENT DAISY JOHNSON. YOUR DAUGHTER IS--
OH, NO.
SHE'S OVERTHROWN THE GOVERNMENT OF LATVERIA AND DECLARED HERSELF ITS SOVEREIGN LEADER.
SAY WHAT NOW?

MA'AM, I HAVE TO ASK YOU, WERE YOU AWARE OF YOUR DAUGHTER'S PLANS TO OVERTHROW AND TAKE CONTROL OF THE SOVEREIGN MONARCHY OF LATVERIA?
NO.
SHE NEVER MENTIONED ANYTHING?
I DO FEEL I WOULD REMEMBER THAT.
UH...
MA'AM, AS HER ONLY LIVING RELATIVE, DO YOU CONSIDER YOURSELF A MEMBER OF MISS WILLIAMS' ROYAL FAMILY?
AND IS YOUR INTENTION FOR THIS PROPERTY TO BE APPROPRIATED AS AN EMBASSY TO LATVERIA?
I THINK I NEED MY LAWYER.

LATVERIA.
WHERE'S LUCIA VON BARDAS?
I'M FREAKING YOU OUT.
ONLY COMPLETELY.
I SAID YOU WOULD.
I BEAT THE BAD GUY.
SURE.
SHE WAS TRYING TO TAKE OVER THIS COUNTRY AND THROW IT AT YOU.
SO I TOOK IT AWAY FROM HER.
DID I DO SOMETHING WRONG?
YOU OVERTHREW A GOVERNMENT.
I DON'T WANT TO UNDERMINE THE ACHIEVEMENT, BUT IT'S REALLY--IT'S NOT MUCH OF A GOVERNMENT.
BAM BAM BAM BAM BAM BAM
BOOM
DEATH TO OPPRESSION!
GIVE US BACK OUR HOME!
HEY!
NO!
WE'RE NOT DOING THIS!
AGENTS, FALL BACK!

NO!
HEY!
EVERYBODY SETTLE DOWN.

HEY, THEY'RE JUST KIDS AND THEY'RE MAD ABOUT EVERYTHING AND THEY'RE PROBABLY RIGHT.
HEY! NO!
STOP!
I MEAN IT.
DROP THE WEAPON OR I'M TAKING YOURS AWAY, TOO!

CAN ANYBODY TRANSLATE THAT FOR ME?

TELL THEM THEY'RE NOT ARRESTED.
ILASDJ DFVIA SUDFBIVAFIEB.
WE UNDERSTAND THEIR FRUSTRATION AND WE'RE TRYING TO GET...
GAEGRE RER REG EEROTOB.
...TO A SOLUTION ON OUR END, SO JUST BE A LITTLE PATIENT.
THETHY RETUHONION FHIHI.
OKAY?
OKAY?
DID YOU TRANSLATE EXACTLY WHAT I SAID?
YES.
DO THEY NOT UNDERSTAND THAT THEY CAN GO?
I THINK YOU STARTLED THEM.
YUP.
SOMETHING YOU WANT TO SAY, GENERAL?
YOU ARE A PECULIAR YOUNG WOMAN.
YOU ARE A GROWN MAN THAT CALLS HIMSELF THE GREEN BEAR.
MY MEN CALL ME THAT BECAUSE OF MY WARTIME RECORD.
SO!
SO.
WHERE IS LUCIA VON BARDAS?
OH, YEAH, COME!

SO TONY A.I. HACKED HER FORCE-FIELD GENERATORS AND TURNED THEM ON HER.
SHE'S BEEN **REALLY** OBNOXIOUS ABOUT IT EVER SINCE.
YOU ARE A **CANCER UPON MY PEOPLE.**
SEE, NOT **ONE** NICE THING.
NOT ONE.
LUCIA **VON BARDAS,** YOU ARE HEREBY OFFICIALLY UNDER S.H.I.E.L.D. ARRES FOR THE UNPROVOKED ATTACK ON THE SMITHSONIAN.

UNPROVOKED?
YOU ARE ***FUNNY.***
YOU CAN TELL YOURSELF ALL ABOUT IT IN THE LITTLE HOLE YOU'RE GOING TO LIVE IN FOR THE REST OF YOUR LIFE.
YOU WILL WATCH YOUR COUNTRY BURN TO THE GROUND!
AND THE REST OF THE WORLD WILL LAUGH AS--!
OH, HEY, LADY, BEFORE YOU GET A REAL HEAD OF MONOLOGUE STEAM GOING...
...REMEMBER A **TEENAGER** JUST KICKED YOUR ASS IN HOMEMADE ARMOR.

THERE ARE VAST INTERNATIONAL COMPLICATIONS THAT GO BACK DECADES, COMPLICATIONS THAT HAVE SO--
RIRI, THAT IS THE GREEN BEAR.
THAT WAS THEN, THIS IS NOW.
NOW, WHAT I TOLD THESE FINE PEOPLE WAS--

GENERAL KARADICK. YES.
I HAVE GOOGLE IN THIS SUIT AND EVERYTHING.
HA!
DID YOU GOOGLE THE PART WHERE HE IS LEADING A HARDLINE MILITARY OVERTHROW OF THIS ENTIRE REGION?

ACTUALLY, TO HEAR HIM TELL IT, HE AND HIS MEN FELT ABANDONED BY THE WORLD AFTER DOOM UP AND LEFT THE COUNTRY.
AND WITH NO ONE TO TURN TO, THEY TURNED TO EACH OTHER.
AND WITH NO RESOURCES OR HELP THEY WERE FORCED TO TAKE A HARD-LINE MILITARY STANCE BECAUSE THERE WAS NO OTHER SUBSTANTIVE RECOURSE--
RIRI--

DID I GET ANY OF THAT WRONG?
NO.

SO, ALTHOUGH YOU FEEL THREATENED, THEY FEEL ABANDONED.
BOTH PRETTY LEGITIMATELY.
IT SEEMS LIKE A COMMUNICATION PROBLEM. PRETTY MUCH.
I HAVE OFFERED TO SIT DOWN WITH S.H.I.E.L.D.
ON NUMEROUS OCCASIONS.
YOU WERE JUST HARBORING A TERRORIST!

I COULD HAVE BLACK-CLOUDED THE AREA.
I COULD HAVE HAD THIS WHOLE COUNTRY GO DARK.
I THOUGHT YOU WOULD.
BUT YOU *DIDN'T.*
MAYBE *YOU* WANT THIS, TOO.

OKAY, YOUR MAJESTY...
...WHAT CAN I DO FOR *YOU?*
LET'S START WITH THE BIG STUFF...
HOLY $#@%

FINAL ☆☆☆☆

DAILY BUGLE®

SINCE 1897 ☆☆☆☆
$1.00 (in NYC)
$1.50 (outside city)

NEW YORK'S FINEST DAILY NEWSPAPER

LATVERIA TO HOLD FIRST FREE ELECTIONS

NEW HOTNESS IRONHEART SEALS THE IMPOSSIBLE DEAL?

HOW OLD IS SHE?

THEY CALL THEMSELVES

THE DEFENDERS!

FIND OUT WHY!

CHICAGO.
OH! GOOD EVENING, YOUNG LADY!
HEY, MOM.
I'M FREAKING OUT!
IT WAS CRAZY AND I TOTALLY ACTED LIKE NO BIG DEAL, BUT--ALL I KEPT THINKING WAS... SCHOOLS.
YEAH, AGENTS VISITING THE HOUSE...
DID YOU EVEN DECIDE IF YOU'RE GOING TO WORK FOR STARK, OR GO BACK TO M.I.T. OR BECOMING A FULL-TIME SUPER HERO?
OH, YEAH!
I DID.
I HAVE SEEN THE FUTURE!

S THERE NNER? I LD EAT MY N FOOT.
I'VE BEEN YING ALL OVER THE PLACE.
UM, SWEETIE, THIS S.H.I.E.L.D. AGENT CAME BY THE HOUSE AND SAID YOU TOOK OVER A COUNTRY.
BABY.
I GAVE IT BACK.
SCHOOLS.
THERE ARE GOING TO BE SCHOOLS THERE AGAIN.
THEY DIDN'T HAVE SCHOOLS.
BUT AFTER TODAY, THEY ALL GET TO GO TO SCHOOL.
YOU'RE FIFTEEN YEARS OLD.
YOU TOLD ME I COULD DO ANYTHING.
YOU SAID IT VERY CLEARLY.
SNIFF
BUT, MOM, THINGS ARE GOING TO GET A LITTLE DICIER NOW.
MORE PEOPLE ARE GOING TO KNOW WHO I AM, AND I THINK WE MIGHT HAVE TO MOVE.
OR SOMETHING.

11

MY NAME IS FRIDAY.
I AM THE PERSONAL ARTIFICIAL ASSISTANT TO TONY STARK.
I RUN THE DAY-TO-DAY GLOBAL OPERATIONS OF STARK INDUSTRIES.
TONY STARK HAS BEEN IN A MEDICALLY INDUCED COMA FOR WHAT I CONSIDER TO BE AN UNCOMFORTABLY LONG TIME.
I HAVE COMPLETE ENCYCLOPEDIC KNOWLEDGE OF HUMAN MEDICINE AND BIOLOGY, AND I'M WORRIED IF SOMETHING ISN'T DONE SOON, THERE MAY BE NO COMING BACK FROM THIS.
RIRI WILLIAMS IS TURNING OUT TO BE A FINE SUPER HERO. IRONHEART IS A BIG WIN.
BUT TONY STARK LEFT BEHIND THE BIRTH MOTHER HE RECENTLY REUNITED WITH-- AND A COMPANY, FRIENDSHIPS AND RELATIONSHIPS THAT DESPERATELY NEED HIM.
I'M WORRIED.
AND THAT'S NOT IN MY PROGRAMMING.

...THAT WHEN THEY FIRST KNOCKED ON THE ORPHANAGE DOO THE PEOPLE INSIDE OPENED IT, HANDED THEM THE BABY AND CLOSED THE DOOR.
AND THAT IS ALL THEY EVER KNEW ABOUT THIS BABY.
BUT HERE I AM WITH A SMORGASBORD OF CLIPS AND FOOTAGE OF THIS MAN IN ALMOST EVERY SITUATION.
I CAN LITERAL WATCH H GROW UP.
CAN I TELL YOU SOMETHING I'VE BEEN DYING TO TELL YOU AND BASICALLY EVERYONE?
BEFORE HE HIRED ME TO BE HIS EXECUTIVE ASSISTANT, I HAD MET TONY STARK BEFORE.
DID HE NOT REMEMBER MEETING YOU WHEN HE HIRED YOU?
HE HAD NO IDEA WE SPENT THE NIGHT TOGETHER.

WOW.
IT'S NICE THAT YOU HAVE SO MUCH FOOTAGE OF HIM.
I WAS JUST THINKING THAT, MJ.
CAN I JOIN YOU FOR LUNCH?
OF COURSE, DARLING.
I WAS THINKING ABOUT THIS WOMAN I WAS IN A BAND WITH ABOUT 20 YEARS AGO.
SHE ADOPTED A BOY AND SHE TOLD ME...
EVERYTHING I MISSED WHEN I GAVE THE BOY AWAY.
AND YOU GET TO REWATCH THINGS THAT YOU SAW ON TV NOT KNOWING THIS WAS YOUR SON.
TRUE.
WOW.
EXCUSE ME?
GOT YOUR ATTENTION...

"SO, IN MY YOUTH, I WAS AN INTERNATIONAL RUNWAY MODEL..."
"YOU DON'T HAVE TO SAY THAT LIKE YOU'RE EMBARRASSED."
"I DON'T. I'M NOT.
"IT'S JUST A WEIRD THING TO SAY OUT LOUD.
"'HI, I'M SOMEONE WHO USED TO TRADE ON HER GOOD LOOKS.'"
"THIRTY YEARS AGO, I HAD THE NUMBER ONE SONG AROUND THE WORLD. AND IN IT I LISTED ALL THE MEN I HAD BEEN WITH."
"WELL, ANYWAY, I WAS YOUNG, I WAS IN MILAN FOR THE FIRST TIME AND I WAS SCARED OUT OF MY MIND BECAUSE...
"...WELL, AS YOU KNOW FROM WATCHING ANYTHING THAT EVER AIRED ON THE *BRAVO* CHANNEL--
"--THE RUNWAY ITSELF IS THE MOST SANE PART OF THE WHOLE PLACE.
"THE REST WAS CRAZY.
"AND THAT WAS BEFORE TONY STARK BARGED IN...

"I WISH I COULD TELL YOU THAT THIS WAS THE FIRST TIME SOME SUPER HERO CRASHED INTO MY LIFE AND RUINED MY MOMENT...

"SPIDER-MAN DID THIS TO ME ABOUT 700 TIMES.
"LONG STORY.
"NOTHING TO DO WITH THIS.

NUAAGGH!

WOOF! ALL RIGHT!
WELL, HI, EVERYBODY!
SORRY ABOUT THIS.
IS THERE AN AFTER-PARTY?

WOW!
WOO!
IRON MAAAAAAAAN!
CLAPCLAPCLAPCLAPCLAPCLAPCLAPCLAPCLAP

TALK TO MY AGENT.

MY AGENT HANDLES THAT.

I'M PRETTY SURE THAT'S ILLEGAL.

"AND THERE HE WAS."
AND THERE YOU ARE.
I AM *VERY* SORRY FOR INTERRUPTING YOUR PERFORMANCE THIS EVENING.
"WHAT DID HE WANT?"
"WHAT DID HE *WANT?*

DID ANYONE EVER TELL YOU YOU SHOULD BE A MODEL?
I'M TONY STARK.
CUTE.
MARY JANE WATSON.
I KNOW.
WHAT DO YOU KNOW?
I KNOW YOU'RE A QUEENS GIRL MAKING YOUR WAY IN THE BIG, BAD WORLD.
AND *HERE* YOU ARE...IN MILAN. KICKING ASS. MAKING YOUR WAY.
UNTIL SOME STUPID AVENGER BODYGUARD CAME IN AND RUINED IT.
KTANG
"THIS WAS BACK WHEN TONY PRETENDED IRON MAN WAS A DIFFERENT GUY...HIS BODYGUARD.
"REMEMBER THAT?
IRON MAN TOLD ME WHAT HAPPENED.
I FELT BAD.
"DID ANY OF US EVER FALL FOR THAT?
I THOUGHT THE LEAST I COULD DO IS COME DOWN HERE, BUY THE YOUNG INGENUE A DRINK...

BECAUSE MY HONEST IS KIND OF GARBAGE TERRIBLE.
IT'S A SHALLOW, CONFUSED, DARK PLACE...

AND IT'S A LITTLE DRUNK.

BECAUSE IT'S SHALLOW, CONFUSED AND... YOU GET IT.

"I CAN'T TELL YOU WHY I DIDN'T LEAVE.
"IT WASN'T THE MONEY OR THE FAME.
"ALMOST EVERYONE THERE HAD ONE OR THE OTHER OR BOTH.

"THERE WAS SOMETHING ELSE.
"HE WASN'T HITTING ON ME.
"ANYMORE.
"IT'S LIKE HE CAME THERE SPECIFICALLY TO HIT ON ME, BUT THEN HE GOT THERE, AND..."
DO YOU LIKE YOUR DAD?

NOT PARTICULARLY.
Y'HAVE A MEAN DAD?
YEAH.
ME TOO.
HE WAS SOOOO MAD AT THE WORLD, AND MY GENERAL EXISTENCE WASN'T HELPING HIM GET OVER IT.

HE SEES YOU STANDING THERE AND INSTEAD OF SEEING LEGACY...
...ALL HE SEES ARE MISSED OPPORTUNITIES.
@#$% YOU, HOWARD.

I LEFT HOME THE SECOND I COULD.
SO DID I.
YEAH, BUT YOU DID IT WITH A BIG DUFFEL BAG FULL OF CASH.
ONLY TO BUY THINGS.

BUT LOOK AT YOU NOW...YOU'RE OUT HERE DOING IT.
SO ARE YOU.
AM I?

YOU DRINK MORE THAN ANYONE I HAVE EVER SEEN, AND I *MIGHT* BE IRISH.
ALCOHOL AFFECTS ME DIFFERENTLY THAN MOST PEOPLE.
REALLY? ARE YOU INHUMAN?

NO.
A MUTANT?
NO.
IT'S JUST DIFFERENT FOR ME.
SEE, THAT SOUNDS A *BIT* LIKE SOMETHING YOU SAY WHEN YOU WANT TO DRINK AND EVERYONE ELSE CAN GO TO HELL.

IT IS.
HONESTY.
NICE.
THANK YOU.
WHAT? IS IT THE STRESS OF BEING IRON MAN?

I'M NOT IRON MAN.
HE'S IRON MAN.
DO YOU THINK PEOPLE REALLY BELIEVE THAT'S NOT YOU?
44 PERCENT OF THE U.S. THINKS IT'S NOT ME.
YOU POLLED IT?

PLEASE!
I'M NOT SO ARROGANT THAT I DO MY OWN POLLING.
THE NEW YORK TIMES DID.
I AM THINKING OF GROWING MY HAIR OUT--WHAT DO YOU THINK?

YOU CAN FLY?
WELL, IT'S THE SUIT MOSTLY, BUT...
IF I COULD FLY...I WOULD JUST GO DO THAT.
I TRY NOT TO FLY DRUNK.

ANYONE CAN DRINK.
I'D JUST FLY.
I DRINK BECAUSE--
YOU WANT TO.

YEAH.

JUST LIKE MY DAD.

I REALLY CAME HERE TO SAY HI TO YOU AND APOLOGIZE FOR INTERRUPTING YOUR SHOW.
I KNOW.
I DIDN'T-- I DIDN'T REALIZE YOU WERE...

NOT SOMEONE YOU CAN JUST POUNCE ON.

YEAH.
SORRY.
DON'T BE.
YOU CAN GO.
I WON'T TELL ANYONE.

YOU HATE ME.

I DON'T THINK I'VE MET *YOU* YET.

GOOD NIGHT, MARY.
YOU REALLY **ARE** SPECIAL.
THAT WAS A STUPID THING TO SAY, BUT IT IS WHAT I WAS THINKING.
HONESTLY.

"YOU MET HIM AND HE DOESN'T EVEN REMEMBER..."

OH, HEY GUYS...
HEY, RIRI WILLIAMS. LOOKING ALL AMAZING!
IS THAT THE QUEEN OF LATVERIA, FLYING DOWN HERE TO TAL TO THE LITTLE PEOPLE?
RETIRED QUEEN OF LATVERIA.
WHAT ARE YOU GUYS DOING?
YOU HANDLED THAT WHOLE SITUATION PRETTY GREAT.
LUNCH.
MANY JANE WAS JUST TELLING ME HOW MY YOUNG, PUNK, DRUNK OF A SON ONCE HIT ON HER AT A PARTY.
DID YOU GUYS--?
RIRI!
IT DOES HAPPEN.
THAT'S SO FUNNY--YOU KNOW, I MET TONY BEFORE, TOO.
BEFORE WHEN?
YOU'RE SIX YEARS OLD.
DO YOU GUYS REMEMBER THE SKRULLS?

"I REMEMBER IT WAS THE DAY MY SOON-TO-BE STEPDAD DECIDED HE WANTED TO BE MY STEPDAD, AND TOOK ME OUT FOR THE FIRST OF WHAT WOULD BE MANY AWESOME, CHILL DADDY-DAUGHTER DATES.
"IF YOU EVER HAVE A DAUGHTER, I HIGHLY RECOMMEND THEM! THEY ARE THERAPEUTIC AND JUST EMPOWERING, IN A WEIRD WAY.
"ANYWAY, HE WAS TRYING TO WIN ME OVER AND I WAS EAGER TO LET HIM.
claire's
"IT WAS A GREAT DAY.
"MY FIRST RATED R MOVIE (A COMEDY).
"BUT SOMETHING WAS GOING ON.
Shop
"THERE WAS THIS REALLY WEIRD VIBE COMING FROM OUTSIDE AND NO ONE SEEMED ABLE TO TALK ABOUT IT.
"WE PEEKED OUT AND...

"...ALIEN INVASION.
"THE SKRULLS.
"THE SHAPE-SHIFTING SKRULLS HAD COME TO TAKE EARTH FOR THEMSELVES.
"YOU GUYS REMEMBER THAT? SURE.
"UP UNTIL THAT MOMENT IT WAS THE CRAZIEST THING I HAD EVER SEEN.
"THEN I TURNED AROUND...

"MAN, MY NEW STEPDAD DIDN'T EVEN *THINK*.
"HE JUST GRABBED ME RIGHT OFF MY FEET *AND RAN*.
"I THINK THAT'S WHY IT TOOK ME A SECOND TO FIGURE OUT...
"...WE WEREN'T ON THE GROUND ANYMORE.

HELL OF A DAY FOR IT.

"I DON'T THINK I SAID ANYTHING.

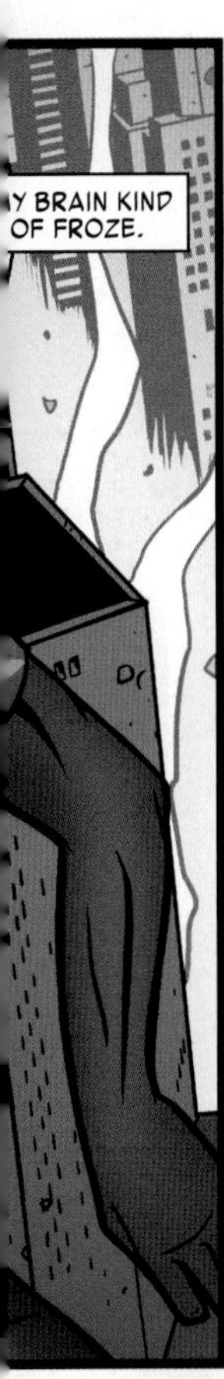
Y BRAIN KIND
OF FROZE.

IT'S PROBABLY SAFER INSIDE, BUT AT THIS MOMENT, WHO THE HELL KNOWS?!
"I REMEMBER BEING SO IMPRESSED WITH HIS ABILITY TO SKILLFULLY DROP US OFF WITHOUT MESSING UP HIS TRAJECTORY.
"ALSO, HIS RIGHT BOOT WASN'T WORKING PROPERLY AND STILL...WOW.

"I LIVE IN CHICAGO. NOT NEW YORK.
"NEW YORK IS LOUSY WITH THIS STUFF...

HIS BOOT IS GLITCHING!
WHAT?
THE ROCKET THRUSTERS ON HIS LEFT BOOT, HE'S GLITCHY!
WELL, HE SEEMS OKAY TO ME!

ACTUALLY, I THINK I KNOW HOW TO FIX THAT.
"I NEVER MENTIONED IT BECAUSE IT'S NOT LIKE IT'S A SPECIAL THING FOR HIM.
"'HEY, REMEMBER THAT LITTLE GIRL AND HER DAD YOU SAVED? NO?'
"'DOESN'T RING A BELL BECAUSE YOU DO THAT LITERALLY FIFTY TIMES A DAY.'

"RIGHT, FRIDAY?
"DOESN'T STARK DO STUFF LIKE THAT EVERY SINGLE DAY?"

OH, I AM **GLAD** YOU ASKED.

TONY STARK HAS SOME SECRETS.

SHOCK!

SECRETS I'M NOT ALLOWED TO REVEAL UNLESS THERE IS SOME STATE OF EMERGENCY.

BUT TONY STARK **IS** IN A COMA AND I DO BELIEVE **THAT** CONSTITUTES AN EMERGENCY.

CAN YOU SHOW US OR NOT, FRIDAY?

AMANDA, YOU ARE NOW IN CHARGE OF THE COMPANY AND ALL ITS ASSETS.

IF YOU WANT TO SEE THE SECRET TONY STARK FILES, ALL YOU HAVE TO DO IS ASK.

FRIDAY, CAN I ***PLEASE*** SEE THE SECRET TONY STARK FILES?

WHY YES, MA'AM.

WHOA, FRIDAY?

UH, WHAT'S HAPPENING?

WE'RE IN A KICKASS VIRTUAL REALITY ARCHIVE.

HAVE ***YOU*** EVER BEEN IN ONE BEFORE?

NO.

THEN HOW DO YOU ***KNOW*** THAT?

I READ.

WHAT IS THAT?
TONY PAYS FOR CRIMINAL REHABILITATION.
ALMOST HIS ENTIRE ROGUES' GALLERY--HIS TERM--IS UNDER TREATMENT AT SOME FACILITY.
TONY ANONYMOUSLY PAYS FOR THEIR THERAPY.
OF COURSE, THE CRIMINALS DON'T KNOW IT.
IF THEY KNEW TONY STARK WAS PAYING, THEY'D NEVER ACCEPT IT.
HE FIGHTS THEM AND THEN HE TRIES TO REHABILITATE THEM?
WELL, AS HE IS FOND OF SAYING: HE WOULD RATHER PAY THE BILL THAN GET PUNCHED IN THE FACE AGAIN.
WAIT, IS HE HUGGING BABIES?
OH, YEAH-- WELL, AMANDA IN PARTICULAR, I THINK YOU'LL LOVE THIS.
SO, IN LOOKING FOR YOU, HIS BIRTH MOTHER, WE VISITED A FEW INTERNATIONAL ADOPTION SERVICES AND ORPHANAGES.
THEY, OF COURSE, ALL NEEDED MORE.
STARK TOOK HIS ENTIRE PERSONAL FOUNDATION AND PUT IT TOWARD FUNDING AS MANY ORPHANAGES AS HE COULD.
PARTICULARLY THE ONES IN TROUBLED AREAS.
HE LIKES TO VISIT.
AND HE HUGS THE BABIES?

THEY NEED TO BE HELD.
HE HOLDS THEM.
HE JUST GOES AROUND THE WORLD AND HOLDS BABIES.
WHEN HE HAS TROUBLE SLEEPING.
WHICH IS A LOT.
MY BOY.
FRIDAY, THE ORPHANAGES.
MAKE SURE THEY HAVE EVERYTHING THEY NEED. COMPUTERS, TOYS, REAL FOOD...
I ALSO-- I WANT PEOPLE TO KNOW. CAN WE PUT MY SON'S NAME ON THESE DONATIONS?
ARE THEY DONATIONS? GIFTS? A FOUNDATION?
IF HE'S PAYING FOR KIDS TO HAVE A FUTURE, YEAH, LET THE WORLD KNOW.
FRIDAY?
FRIDAY?
IS SHE FROZEN?
THAT'S NOT TECHNICALLY POSSIBLE. A HOLOGRAM IS A SELF-REPLICATING--
SHOULD WE REBOOT HER?
SHE'S NOT A PHONE.
FRIDAY?

TONY STARK.
YES.
I WANT **HIS** NAME ON THE--
TONY STARK.
SEARCHING...
FRIDAY?
HE'S GONE.
HE'S--
DEAD?
NO. GONE.

GONE WHERE?
NEXT: THE SEARCH FOR TONY STARK!

11 LETTER BY BRIAN MICHAEL BENDIS

Hi. It's Brian. I've been writing IRON MAN for a few years but this is my first letter column. I wanted to take a moment to talk about this issue. We have some VERY special guest artists with us, whom I will get to in a minute, but I wanted to tell you about who this issue is dedicated to and why.

I live in Portland, Oregon. When you move to a new neighborhood, one of the big X factors is your neighbors. Who will they be? Will we like each other? Will we go to war over a shrub? We had just left one of those great old neighborhoods where we became friends and family with almost all of our neighbors. We were worried about missing out on that special feeling.

That's when we met our NEW across-the-street neighbors of the last seven years...the Cheeks. Let me tell you about Dick Cheek. Make the jokes. He's heard them all.

His name is Richard Cheek and I soon found out he's a real super hero.

Dick and his wife, Helen, both in their eighties, and their eight adult children (!) are just amazing people. Great positive energy EVERYWHERE they go. Big on community. BIG on helping out anyone who needs a little help, be it through church, community organizing or just looking out. Almost to an unbelievable degree.

I could literally spend this entire issue listing kindnesses I know of or witnessed them do. It's exhaustive. It's crazy. Who is this nice? For all these years, they did us neighborly kindnesses that we never asked for. Did I say he was in his eighties? Yes. But you couldn't tell. Such a zest for life.

It just so happened, after the first time I had met him, I had to run off to a Marvel retreat. In the cab on the way to the airport, the cab driver looked at Dick's house, turned to me and said: "Oh my God! You live across the street from the Cheeks. He saved my father's life in the war. He's a genuine war hero. I wouldn't be here if not for him. Has he ever told you about that?"

The next time I got a chance to ask him, he blew it off warmly and just chuckled. Then, I heard from his children that he was the real deal.

I will honor his service by not speaking of things he clearly did not want spoken of...but he was a war hero.

As our relationship developed over the years, he told me that his priest happened to be a huge comic book fan and wanted to talk to me about the spirituality of comics over dinner. The Jew in me expected a "hip" younger priest into SPIDER-MAN or GUARDIANS OF THE GALAXY. You know, for the kids! I was surprised to find this big, gray-haired, Brian-Dennehy-with-a-priest-collar shake my hand and say, "I love ALIAS and *Powers.*" To have a man of the cloth tell you how much he loves your basically rated R work was the beginning of a surreal and spiritually exciting dinner. One of the most fun dinners I've ever had. It changed my work. For the better.

So over the last few years, my wife started including the Cheeks at our semi-regular Friday night dinners. A dinner MOSTLY for our Portland comics peer group. So many of my friends, who just happen to be some of your favorite comic creators, have become big fans and friends of the Cheeks as well.

Well, as it goes, this summer both Helen and Dick started to feel their age. I was at their 65th wedding anniversary party, and they showed a slide show of family, mountain hiking, world travel and real adventure that was awe-inspiring to say the least. When the Cheeks started to slow down you could feel it.

Dick's health started to slip and he had been in hospice for most of the summer. We would visit and Helen would be frustrated that she was in the hospital because Dick needed her...and he said the exact same thing about her. Just heartwarming. My wife and I have been happily married for over 20 years and it gave US relationship goals.

During his time in hospice, Dick came over. He could feel everyone's stress about the situation. He came over just to tell me, "Hey, tell everyone that I'm okay. That I've lived a long and fortunate life. My kids are amazing, my wife loves me and I think I left the world a little better than the way I found it. I'm really okay with everything that's happening now. I'm good to go."

And then he said, after attending dozens of dinners at my house with all of your favorite kind of comic creators, "Hey, did I ever tell you that I was friends with Walt Kelly?"

After seven years of knowing each other, I turned to him and said with an incredulous smile, "No, Dick, I did not know you were friends with one of the greatest cartoonists of all time." He then pulled out the correspondence between the two of them, and the original art that Walt Kelly had given him as a present, and some other insane Walt Kelly memorabilia. I was blown away, and I told our mutual friend, and one of the artists of this issue, Taki Soma--and Taki said, "That's my favorite artist of all time." I guess I'm not surprised, but I am surprised, because when I told Dick, he gave Taki and me his Walt Kelly original art, memorabilia and correspondence.

I didn't want to take it. He has kids. They should have it. I told the sons. They made it very clear that Dick wanted us to have it. I said I could donate it to a library cartoonist archive. I was told no. He wanted us to have it. It might even be why we met, so one of his lifelong prize possessions could have a truly appreciative home.

Seven years and this war-hero super hero never told me he was one of us. Secret nerd!

The reason this specific issue is dedicated to him is that a couple weeks ago, his son walked over just to say hi to my wife and me. Stunned to have just learned this himself, he asked us, "Did you know that my father, when he has time, goes to hospitals and just holds the babies?"

We were as stunned as he was. Who does that? Who does that and doesn't tell anybody?

Yeah, the most unbelievable concept in this issue was based on the true Dick Cheek. I was told this as I was thinking, what's the coolest thing Tony Stark could've done that no one knows he's done? I really wrote that question down for this issue and then Dick's son comes over and drops this on me.

So, inspired, I wrote this issue and I went over and I told them. Of course, he was a little embarrassed, but his wife and his kids were thrilled.

Then this issue started to reveal a fragmented structure, and I thought this gave us this great opportunity to spotlight some different artists for this issue. Stefano was going to need a little bit of a break to get to our big Legacy story next issue anyhow, and I thought this was a great opportunity to join Kelly Sue DeConnick's "Visible Women" Twitter campaign and shine a spotlight on some female creators in this book filled with female voices. And now Taki Soma makes her Marvel Comics debut for an issue especially dedicated to a good friend of both of ours. He gave us something special to keep of his and we wanted to give you something of him.

Kate Niemczyk blew me away with her work on MOCKINGBIRD, and I have been dying to do something with her--and Tom Brevoort, in his travels, showed me the world of Kiichi Mizushima. It's like she fell out of the sky to bring the perfect voice to her chapter. I would like to report that, behind the scenes, Stefano and all the artists had an amazing creative experience. They have been emailing all month. The book was made with love from beginning to end, just like the man the book is dedicated to.

The reason I'm telling you all of this is, about two hours ago, he passed away. In my heart, I hoped that I could give him this issue before he passed, but he passed this morning before it went to print.

I don't know when you'll be reading this, but if you're reading it the day it came out, I think you can agree that the world has been a hot mess lately. One of my personal ways of dealing with the stress of it is knowing that there are people in the world like the Cheeks.

I thought you'd like a reminder, too. They are people who do kindnesses because that's what you're supposed to do. In his honor, today, if you find someone that needs a little kindness, maybe stop and do it. Do that.

Be an honest-to-goodness real super hero like Dick Cheek. A kindness is all it takes.

— BENDIS!

MARCO CHECCHETTO

9 MARY JANE VARIANT

ADI GRANOV

11 VENOMIZED VILLAINS VARIANT

STEFANO CASELLI

ISSUE 8, PAGE 21 ART

STEFANO CASELLI

ISSUE 10, PAGES 4-5 ART

KATE NIEMCZYK

ISSUE 11, PAGE 4 ART